COAST
TO
COAST

COAST
TO
COAST

*SPIRITUAL
LESSONS
from a
BICYCLE
SEAT*

BRYAN RATLIFF

REDEMPTION PRESS

Published by Redemption Press, PO Box 427, Enumclaw, WA 98022.

Toll-Free (844) 2REDEEM (273-3336)

Redemption Press is honored to present this title in partnership with the author. The views expressed or implied in this work are those of the author. Redemption Press provides our imprint seal representing design excellence, creative content, and high-quality production.

978-1-68314-776-3 Soft Cover
978-1-68314-777-0 ePub
978-1-68314-778-7 Mobi

Library of Congress Catalog Number: 2019911915

TABLE OF CONTENTS

In the Beginning . . .

INTRODUCTION

In June 2015 I was blessed with the opportunity of a lifetime—to lead a unique mission team from Clearbrook Baptist Church across America on a bicycle. The twofold purpose of our adventure was to increase gospel awareness throughout the United States of America and to raise money for the building fund of Clearbrook Baptist Church. We left Roanoke, Virginia, on May 27, 2015, to travel to San Diego, California, to begin our cycling journey. Our team cycled approximately 3,000 miles, from San Diego to St. Augustine, Florida, in thirty days. Along the way, we ministered in several churches and communities, fulfilling one of the two reasons for this excursion—to raise gospel awareness throughout the United States of America.

Our missions team consisted of eleven members. Kevin Dunbar and Howard Martin were our drivers, navigators, and mechanics. Dave Schultz, Greg Parsons, Aaron Wallace, and I were the cyclists. David Schultz (Dave's son), Mindy Wallace (Aaron's wife), Hannah Shank, Elisabeth Shank, and Andrea Glovier were part of the support team, helping us with photography, videography, cooking, laundry, shopping, and just about everything else. It was a blessing to see God at work in each of the team members on this trip. At some point, each of them shared their testimony of salvation on the trip and how God changed their life for all eternity.

There are three major cross-country routes listed by the Adventure Cycling Association. They are called the Northern Tier Route, the TransAmerica Trail, and the Southern Tier Route. The Northern Tier spans across most of the northernmost states and is just over 4,000 miles long, from Washington to Maine. The TransAmerica Trail begins in Oregon and spans to Virginia and is about 4,000 miles long. The

Southern Tier starts in San Diego and ends in St. Augustine, Florida, and covers approximately 3,000 miles. Even though it was going to be a little warmer than the other routes, our team decided on the Southern Tier because it was the shortest and was more achievable with our timeline.

This book shares some of the incredible encounters experienced along the way, as well as spiritual lessons gleaned through our fantastic voyage. The Lord has placed it upon my heart to write a book about this epic ride and tell how God worked through us to spread His Word to those who crossed our paths. All royalties and proceeds from this book will be donated to the Clearbrook Baptist Church's building fund. As a token of my appreciation, all who support the cause will receive via email my thirty-day devotional e-book for free by going to www.pastorbryanratliff.com and filling out the form.

An Idea Is Born . . .

CHAPTER 1

How It All Began

∽०∾

THE HISTORY

Growing up in the States, riding a bicycle was a favorite pastime for me, just like it was for nearly every child. When my family would go to Douthat State Park for vacations, I would always take my bike to ride along the trails and to the swimming area. Other than that and occasionally riding to a friend's house during the summer, I didn't ride much, though. I can honestly say that I probably had not ridden 3,000 total miles on a bicycle up to that time in my life.

I've always been active. Playing sports and working out have been my hobbies, but cycling never crossed my mind until after college. After returning home from Bible college and becoming the pastor at Clearbrook Baptist Church, I began going to the gym to play basketball. It was a great way to get a cardio workout. Those pickup games were a ton of fun, but they'd always get heated. Some of the guys were playing like it was the Final Four championship game, and I was like, "Bro, I'm just trying to get some cardio in." Honestly, I was tired of getting elbowed and rolling my ankles, and I was ready for another way of getting in a cardio workout.

That's when it hit me. *Just ride your bike.* When playing basketball, you need to rely on others, but cycling can be done without anyone else and at your convenience. I loved that concept. As a minister, I don't have the luxury of always having a routine schedule. I was living in my parents' house at the time, and I went to the basement and discovered three old Walmart mountain bikes. After analyzing each of them, I chose the best one, but I quickly realized I should just buy a new one. I wasn't ready for a bike-shop purchase, so I went to Walmart and bought a Genesis twenty-nine-inch bike—just the right thing for the streets and trails. I figured that would be a good investment to see if it was worth getting into.

Since I spent the majority of my rides on the road, I wanted to switch from mountain bike tires to some hybrid tires. I'll never forget walking into the bike shop for the first time. It was like bicycle heaven—until I looked at the price tags. Then it became more like bicycle purgatory. Nonetheless, I showed one of the staff members my mountain bike tire and expressed interest in buying some hybrid tires. They showed me exactly what I needed, and it was far less expensive than I had thought. I was amazed at how much faster I could go on the roads with the new hybrid tires.

Zooming down the back roads of Boones Mill, Virginia, on a Walmart mountain bike with hybrid tires at over 40 mph without a helmet probably wasn't the safest idea, but it sure was fun. After continual recommendations from friends and family, I finally bought a helmet. For the record, since that purchase I have always worn a helmet when I ride. Wear your helmet, kids; it will help keep your noggin safe. Needless to say, I was bitten by the cycling bug, and cycling became a standard routine in my cardio workouts. Several of my friends at Clearbrook Baptist Church enjoyed riding bikes too. I began to use cycling as an opportunity to have some fun, get some exercise, and enjoy the camaraderie with fellow believers.

The Inspiration

Since June 2011, our church has experienced growth. We continually praise the Lord for each of the individuals who have put their faith in Christ and have joined our community of believers. The auditorium at our church will seat a maximum of 220 people, but when 150 people are present, it feels pretty crowded. Throughout the past few years, we have discussed and done many things to help promote growth, but our long-term goal was to construct a new building. I began to brainstorm ideas for fundraisers, and I came across some interesting individuals who had used cycling to raise money for charity.

Back in 2014 while listening to Pastor Greg Locke preach on his church's YouTube channel, I heard about his epic ride across America in ten days. He averaged about three hundred miles a day. His cause was to raise money for his church. I thought this was an amazing idea, but I wasn't willing to try doing it in ten days. I decided to reach out to him through email. He graciously and generously offered some advice. While most cyclists discouraged me about my idea of cycling across America in thirty days, he was one of the few to offer encouragement. What inspired me the most about Pastor Locke was the similar vision we shared: he was a fellow pastor seeking to raise finances for his ministry, and he rode across America for his one-year cycling anniversary. My thought was, *If Pastor Locke did it in ten days, then I can do it in thirty.*

As I continued to research, I came across a celebrity named Phil Keoghan who rode across America in 2012. He rode 3,500 miles in forty days, from Los Angeles to New York City, to raise awareness of and funds to benefit the National Multiple Sclerosis Society. In nearly all the cities where he stopped, Phil spoke at meetings to help raise awareness for his cause. Since he was a celebrity, I didn't have the luxury of reaching out to him, but he had posted a documentary about his adventure. I watched it several times, studied it in depth, and modeled our trip after his. The most inspiring part about Phil's journey across America is that he did it at the age of forty. I was twenty-six years old at the time and told myself, *If a forty-year-old can do it, I can do it too.*

While surfing YouTube for other cyclists who pedaled from coast to coast, I came across a lady named Angeline Tan. Her documentary, *Angie across America: Official Documentary*, was incredibly inspiring. In June 2014, at the age of thirty-five, Angie rode four thousand miles in thirty-nine days. She averaged about a hundred miles a day. She didn't set out to raise money for charity, but her story inspired others to dream big. She's known for saying, "If in your heart you believe, you can achieve."[1] She also wrote a book about her adventure that tells more about her journey across the United States. After learning about her story, I told myself, *If Angie can do it, then so can I.*

THE IDEA

After hearing about Pastor Greg Locke, Phil Keoghan, and Angeline Tan, I was extremely inspired to set out on an adventure to pedal across America. However, planning a trip like that is easier said than done. In the summer of 2014, I was leading a mission team to Concord, New Hampshire, to help a recent church plant. It was during that trip that I first suggested the idea of a unique mission trip across the United States of America via bicycle. The team members thought it was a really cool idea, and they seemed very interested. We continued ministering in New Hampshire, and I began to seriously contemplate the logistics of what, in some ways, seemed an insurmountable task.

There were already a few individuals from the church with whom I was riding regularly. We tried to ride once or twice a week, but it didn't always work out. It was a fun time of fellowship for each of us. Dave, Greg, Aaron, and I would cruise around the roads of Roanoke riding old,

[1] Angie attributes the quote to Napoleon Hill: "Truly, as Napoleon Hill inspired me when I was 10, whose quote is the bedrock for my crossing America in 2014, and which continues to hold true for my upcoming race in Ireland: 'Whatever your mind can conceive, and your heart can believe, you can achieve." https://www.angieacrossamerica.com/blog/transatlantic-way-race-race-around-ireland-june-17-2016.

beat-up Walmart bikes, and it was a blast. Greg was the only one who had a nicer bicycle. During those rides, we began to discuss riding across America. Honestly, riding across America for cyclists is what hiking the Appalachian Trail is for hikers. The vast majority of the discussion is just a dream. It rarely ever turns into reality.

I cannot remember why we went out to eat at Rancho Viejo, but I remember each of us being there. Cycling across America became one of our go-to topics. It was about the only thing we could discuss. During that meal, I remember asking Dave, Greg, and Aaron if they would join me if I planned the trip across America. To my surprise, each of them said yes. Even though they said "Yes" out loud, I'm sure they said in their hearts, "There's no way he will plan it." To their surprise, I planned it.

Because the Ladies Fellowship had raised a lot of money for missions and had done so much for our church, I thought it was a good idea to present the idea to them and hear their thoughts before bringing it up in a business meeting. After much preparation, the day came when I presented the official idea to the Ladies Fellowship group at church. I shared with them how our mission team would ride from San Diego to St. Augustine to raise gospel awareness and to raise money for Clearbrook's building fund. After much discussion and numerous questions, they agreed to support the idea. We also discussed it in our deacons-and-trustees meeting, and the trip was officially voted on in the fall of 2014. To my surprise, our church unanimously voted to support it.

I was ecstatic about it, but I was nervous too. *What if we don't raise any money? How will we pay for the expenses? Where will we stay? Will any churches be willing to host us? What if the other guys end up not being able to go? What will we eat?* All these questions and many more will be answered in the pages to come. I am very excited to tell you about this trip and how God taught us some great spiritual lessons along the way.

Beginning at the Beginning . . .

CHAPTER 2

Obstacles Are Opportunities

Problems are going to come, and there's nothing we can do about it. Nobody can escape the obstacles faced in life, but we can use them as leverage to become better people. Obstacles are merely tools God uses to fashion us more into His image. Attempting to avoid the obstacles life brings also causes us to avoid possibilities of magnificent spiritual growth. Obstacles not only help us grow spiritually, but they also make us more mature. I'd like to share with you some of the personal obstacles the team and I faced while pedaling across America and what we learned from them.

∽೦∾

OBSTACLES ARE OPPORTUNITIES TO SUCCEED

"Bryan, come look at the bikers," my dad shouted from the kitchen. I ran from my bedroom as fast as I could to see a gigantic group of professional cyclists zooming down the road. For some reason, I was fascinated with those guys riding their bicycles. I suppose this was around the time of the Tour DuPont. I remember the feeling of freedom that riding my Walmart mountain bike gave me as a young whippersnapper. Every time I begin to ride my bike, I am taken back to those unforgettable childhood memories.

Cycling certainly has moments full of freedom, but every ride also presents its own share of challenging obstacles. Granted, I definitely wasn't going on long-distance endurance rides as a kid, but even then there were always challenges—from the chain falling off to my feet slipping off the pedals to my shins slamming into the pedals. I remember mapping out a course to my babysitter's house and racing there with some of my friends and getting lapped by them. Trying to keep up with those guys was a large obstacle, but none of that compared to facing the ginormous one of pedaling from sea to shining sea.

You need to understand that I had never owned a road bicycle prior to preparing for this trip. A bicycle with curved handlebars wasn't even a consideration. How in the world was I, along with the three other fellas, going to ride across America? None of us had ever imagined doing something like that before. Would we even make it halfway? These were the constant thoughts going through my mind at first, but I figured out that this was an opportunity for success. *Success* is defined as "the accomplishment of an aim or purpose." I decided we could use this challenging obstacle to greatly succeed.

Overcoming obstacles begins by using them as opportunities to succeed. Setting small goals helps to accomplish big goals. The obstacle of riding across America became the big goal to achieve. In order to fulfill this giant task, I established miniature goals along the way. For example, my goal for every day of the trip was to finish that day. I knew the chances of pedaling every mile across America began by pedaling every mile of Day 1, then Day 2, then Day 3, etc. Believe it or not, this was one of the greatest things for me mentally on this trip. I'd tell myself, *Bryan, just get through this day. All you've got to do is finish today's ride.*

There were many struggles in accomplishing the ride to the top of Emory Pass, but on Sunday, June 7, 2015, I did it. I told myself, *If I can make it to Emory Pass without stopping, then I can go all the way.* We had just finished ministering at the First Baptist Church of Silver City, New Mexico. We quickly ate lunch and then jolted out of town to start our big ascent. Dave, Greg, and I left Silver City not really knowing what to expect. I was somewhat dreading the ride because Emory Pass looked extremely intimidating on the map. Fortunately, just prior to leaving Silver City, we met a cyclist named Christian, who gave us a heads-up about the major climb. I will tell more about meeting him later, but God had certainly orchestrated a divine appointment.

Armed with what we had learned from Christian, we began our climb. Dave rode as far as he could, and then he said to Greg and me, "The mountain is all yours." He rode the rest of the way up in the motor home and then rejoined us at the top for the major descent. Going up Emory Pass wasn't as bad as we had anticipated. We weren't going for any world records. We just took our time going up. There were still twenty-three days left, and we knew the importance of not overexerting ourselves. While traveling up, we stopped a few times to take in the beautiful scenery.

∞•∞

OBSTACLES ARE OPPORTUNITIES TO WORK HARDER

As I hung up the phone, I thought, *Is any church going to host us?* San Diego was our starting point, and I had this epiphany about testifying in a church in every town where we stopped. It was God's providential plan not to have me do this, though, knowing our team couldn't handle a service in every town. I pulled out my laptop, went to the internet browser, and googled "Baptist churches in San Diego." Then I began to call every church I found listed. I started making calls with great enthusiasm, but I ended with much discouragement.

It seemed like every church in San Diego was a large megachurch and wasn't interested in hosting us. When I made these calls, I felt like a telemarketer. I knew I had less than ten seconds to grab their attention. I'll share more about the details later. Most of the churches around the country that I called were very interested in hearing about what we were doing, but San Diego was a different story. If the churches weren't willing to allow us to serve in their meetings, I asked if it would be possible for us to at least park our motor home on their property and stay the night. One of the ladies I spoke with over the phone told me, "Just so you know, it is illegal in San Diego to park your motor home in a parking lot and sleep in it."

As you could imagine, I was very discouraged about the phone calls in San Diego. After a few moments of prayer, I moved on to the next city, El Centro. I googled "Baptist churches in El Centro, CA." The first church I contacted in that area scheduled us. They said we could spend the night in their gymnasium. Earlier I had been defeated with discouragement, but now I was jumping for joy. You might think I'm exaggerating, but I was literally jumping around the auditorium of Clearbrook Baptist Church shouting praises to the Lord.

Overcome obstacles by using them as inspiration to work harder. The small roadblock of churches not willing to host us in San Diego was discouraging, but I decided I was going to work harder and pray harder for God to open doors. God intervened and blessed the countless hours of contacting churches, pastors, and ministries. For every closed door, God seemed to open a better door for our team to minister. For the record, when I got to San Diego, it became one of my favorite cities that we visited. The beach was amazing and the roads were spectacular.

Another obstacle I faced leading up to riding across America was some of the discouragement from other cyclists. I remember walking into one of the local bike shops, looking around, and buying a few necessary items. I told the cashier what I was planning to do, and I asked if he would be willing to offer any advice. Without hesitation, he looked me directly in the eyes and said, "If it was me, I wouldn't do it."

Although I appreciated the straightforwardness, it was discouraging. At the time, I didn't realize how challenging the trip would be. The guy at the bike shop was just expressing that he never wanted to put his body through such a rigorous task. It was too much riding for him. I was full of discouragement after talking with him. For every person who offered discouraging words, though, it seemed like God brought another person along to give a word of encouragement.

I decided to buy a new and better bike for the trip. After googling different road bikes, I decided I wanted a 2015 Giant Defy Advanced

2 with disc brakes. I went to another local bike shop that sold Giant bicycles. I was browsing around the store, checking out the different road bikes, and one of the staff introduced himself to me. His name was Devin. He had ridden across America a few years earlier, and he offered me much excellent advice and help.

In 2014, when my schedule allowed, I volunteered on Wednesdays at Roanoke Memorial Hospital by playing music at their cancer center, cafeteria, and other locations. It was a blessing to minister through music to those who were facing major trials. Through that opportunity, God allowed me to meet an avid local cyclist named Reid. After hearing my story, Reid gave me an endurance-cycling book that greatly helped during my training. Once I purchased a road bike, Reid offered to take me for a ride around the Bradshaw Loop. It was about a fifty-mile ride. Before this, my longest ride had been about thirty-six miles on the Roanoke River Greenway. Additionally, I didn't have the special cycling shoes yet.

I went with Reid, though, around the Bradshaw Loop. It was a fun ride, but at the end of it, I was toast. Reid shared something that would inspire me for the rest of my training: "Be true to yourself, Bryan." Those words rang in my head continually. That training ride was in the fall of 2014, and I was scheduled to ride across America in June 2015. To say it mildly, I needed some work. If I had embarked on the journey that day, I would have failed miserably. At first I was discouraged by how challenging the ride was, but after talking with Reid, I was motivated to take the training to the next level. I was inspired to overcome this obstacle by working hard.

God's greatest soldiers battle discouragement. From Joseph being forgotten in a prison cell to Elijah's loneliness as a prophet, many of God's greatest warriors faced discouraging moments. If some of the greatest spiritual soldiers throughout the Old and New Testaments have fought discouragement, we will face it too. God offers a word of encouragement in Psalm 55:22: "Cast thy burden upon the LORD, and he shall sustain thee: he shall never suffer the righteous to be moved." Here's a word of encouragement from 1 Peter 5:7: "Casting all your care upon him; for he careth for you." Every time I am discouraged, I go to these two verses in the Bible. Whenever you travel down the road of discouragement, know that God can help you journey through it. Don't give up; just work harder.

∞

Obstacles Are Opportunities to Strengthen Relationships

Obstacles can either hinder or help your relationships. Whenever you live with somebody for an extended period of time, ups and downs are guaranteed. I learned this in college. I went to three different undergraduate Christian colleges, and each of them organized the dormitories differently. I was in one Bible college in northern Indiana where six of us were packed in a small room like a bunch of sardines. The Bible college I attended in Knoxville, Tennessee, had more spacious rooms, but it wasn't uncommon to have ten guys per room. The rooms were large with two walk-in closets, but ten guys in one room had its challenges. I believe those college dormitory days were preparing me for our mission trip across America.

As you can imagine, it is possible to have nine people living in a motor home, but that doesn't mean it should be done. For the majority of the time, we all got along, although there were times when we didn't see eye to eye. When we drove out of the parking lot around 4:00 p.m. on May 27, 2015, we didn't stop, except to get gas, until we arrived in Shamrock, Texas, twenty-four hours later. In theory, it was a great idea, but in practice, it was a horrible decision. We all ended up cranky and exhausted. In fact, if we did this trip all over again, I would not travel like this.

The first night, I slept in the bunk bed above the captain's seat. It was very comfortable, but every time the driver hit the brakes, I felt like I was going to fly off onto the ground. When the driver slowed down, I was forced to instantly raise my arm to the ceiling to keep from falling off. I'm sure I was just anxious and being extra cautious, but I didn't get any sleep that night. After the first day of traveling, we began to sleep better, and once we started cycling, we slept like a bunch of babies.

Throughout the month of June, we faced some disagreements and division. We are Baptists, after all, and unfortunately, Baptists gravitate toward division. All jokes aside, I don't remember all the details of where we were or what exactly happened, but something troubling went down while I was riding solo one day. The division was so severe that some of the team members were planning on going home. The arguments were more than just a debate. When I rode into the campground, a couple of the team members informed me of the situation. I understood why some were going to leave, but my prayer was that our team would work through these dilemmas.

To God be the glory, our team was able to work through this obstacle and other similar problems along the way. We had eleven team members, and it's a miracle we're all still friends. If our mission team was able to work through our problems, come together, and become unified, then anybody can do it. Listen to the words of Psalm 133:1: "Behold, how good and how pleasant it is for brethren to dwell together in unity!" There is no division in the body of Christ that God cannot fix. There is no problem in the local church that God cannot resolve. Division is going to happen. The apostle Paul encountered it and was affected by it, but how we handle division reflects the status of our relationship with Christ. God doesn't hate division in and of itself, but He does abhor those who sow discord in the body of believers (Proverbs 6:19). When the obstacle of division comes, allow it to strengthen your relationship with Christ.

Another obstacle our team faced was when I miscalculated the sleeping arrangements. As you might think, this became quite an issue. Before the trip, I visited Howard at his home to take a look at the nice motor home he generously allowed our team to use. I remember walking through the motor home calculating how many people could sleep in it. "We could sleep three girls in the back room, two people in the bunk beds, two people on the table, two people on the couch, and one person above the driver's seat. That's ten people. We're in great shape," I said. We also had a couple of team members express interest in sleeping outside in a tent. After hearing that, I didn't give it much more thought.

Our team consisted of eleven people: seven guys and four girls. Only seven of the team members were able to do the entire trip. Two of the ladies, Hannah and Andrea, flew back home when we got to Del Rio, Texas. Aaron and Mindy met us in Leakey, Texas. When we left Roanoke, Virginia, we had six men and three ladies. Halfway through, we had seven men and two ladies. When making the calculations for sleeping arrangements for the transition of new team members, I didn't factor in that we would have one more guy and one less girl. Needless to say, I totally blew it. I guess I was focused on planning everything else for the trip and overlooked this area.

If I had the chance to make this trip all over again, I'd do it in a heartbeat. It was a blast. One of the things I would change, though, is how many people we took. As much as I enjoyed everyone's company, too many people went with us. Even though the motor home could theoretically sleep ten, ten was entirely too many bodies. Realistically, only one person could sleep on the couch, and only one person could sleep on the table. With God's help, we were able to make some adjustments and work through this obstacle. I believe this forced us to strengthen our friendships, expand our relationships, and draw us closer to Christ.

❧

OBSTACLES ARE OPPORTUNITIES TO DEVELOP CHRISTLIKE ATTITUDES

Attitudes during challenging obstacles can certainly reflect and sometimes determine the direction of our relationship with Christ. I'd like to say that everyone's attitude along the journey was positive, but that wasn't always the case. One of my pet peeves is when people are not punctual. This trip showed me that not everyone has the same pet peeve. When I first got my driver's license, my dad gave me a curfew of 11:00 p.m. I walked into the house one evening at 11:03 p.m. My dad was right there in the kitchen waiting for me. The first thing he said to me was "Hand me your keys. You're grounded for two weeks." I did everything I could to wiggle out of the situation, but my father did not budge. That's probably one of the greatest lessons my parents taught me during my adolescent years.

In our meetings leading up to the journey across the United States, we decided to get an early start every day so we wouldn't have to ride through the hot part of the day. In theory, it was a fantastic idea. It worked great for the first few days, but due to our physical conditioning (or lack thereof) and the resulting exhaustion, we were not able to leave as early each day as we had planned. None of us had ever ridden across America before, and we didn't really know what we were getting ourselves into. There were some days I'd tell everybody we were going to leave around 9:00 a.m., but we didn't leave until two or three hours later.

My pet peeve for lack of punctuality was tried and tested, but I soon learned I needed to give everyone the benefit of the doubt because of how drained our bodies were. To help matters, on the days we had obligations that required leaving at a certain time, I let the team know ahead of time when I planned to leave, telling them that if they wanted to join me, they could let me know and I would make sure they were awake. Some of those early mornings were done solo. I believe (and hope) I was very gracious in handling these issues throughout the entire trip.

OBSTACLES ARE OPPORTUNITIES TO OVERCOME FEAR

I'm not much of a person to get scared or afraid. Whenever I've gone to a haunted house, I have found them to be more humorous than anything else. Everything about this trip, however, made me anxious, afraid, and fearful. I was afraid that something would go wrong that would detain us and keep us from completing the task. I was anxiously worried about letting people down. I was fearful of the unknown that we would encounter. From every perspective and every angle, I was afraid. I relied on 2 Timothy 1:7 to help calm my nerves and worries. It says, "For God hath not given us the spirit of fear; but of power, and of love, and of a sound mind." Whenever fear consumed my thoughts, I quoted this verse.

We all have fears. Whether you're afraid of the dark or afraid of where you'll spend eternity, we all have fears. We can overcome the obstacle of fear with God's divine assistance. Many of the characters throughout the Scriptures had fears just like us. They were humans just like us. They had fears, anxieties, and worries and were frightened just like us, but God helped them.

Abraham and Sarah overcame the fear of having a child late in life. Isaac overcame the fear of being sacrificed on an altar. Jacob overcame the fear of his brother Esau. Joseph overcame the fear of despair in prison. Moses overcame the fear of speaking to the Israelites and Pharaoh. Joshua overcame his fear of conquering Jericho. Gideon overcame his fear of the Midianites. David overcame the giant of Gath. Elijah overcame loneliness when God showed him other believers. Jonah overcame his refusal to go to Nineveh. Daniel overcame the lions in the den. Shadrach, Meshach, and Abednego overcame their fear of the fiery furnace.

Mary overcame the false accusation. Joseph overcame the false accusations. Simon Peter overcame his fear by walking on the water with Jesus. James was an overcomer by being martyred for the faith. Stephen overcame his fear by preaching the gospel to the Jewish people. John overcame his fear to author many of the books in the New Testament. Philip was an overcomer when he witnessed to the Ethiopian eunuch.

Thomas overcame doubt when he saw Christ after the resurrection. Paul was an overcomer by becoming one of the greatest missionaries of all time. Mary Magdalene overcame her fear by sharing the news of Christ's resurrection. If God helped them become overcomers, then surely He can help you overcome any fear you're facing.

CHAPTER 3
Preparation Is King

The key to obtaining success is preparation. Planning may sound too professional for some, but the busier an individual becomes, the more necessary it is to prepare for what is to come. What gets scheduled gets done. Perhaps you could just ride your bicycle across America, but it required serious preparation for me. If it weren't for all the planning that took place beforehand, I do not believe we would have been able to complete our escapade. Preparation was key.

PERFECT PRACTICE PROMOTES PERFECT PERFORMANCE

Athletes take their training schedule very seriously. They make necessary sacrifices to obtain high levels of physical fitness. Rigorous training schedules are designed to equip the athlete for greater odds of success. Many athletes treat their training like ritualistic religious exercises. An Olympic runner is not birthed overnight. It takes many years of hard work, dedication, determination, and sacrifice to win a gold medal. NBA all-stars didn't just pick up a basketball and say, "I think I'll try out for the Lakers today." No matter if it's the NHL, MLB, NASCAR, or any other sport, achieving the highest level of success begins by showing up for practice every day with a willingness to work hard.

If you've never been on a long-distance endurance bicycle ride, then you really have no clue how strenuous this is on the human body. This is not an adventure you could successfully finish without adequate preparation. Even those who logged many miles in the saddle leading up to a cross-country cycling tour wish they would have prepared more. That was certainly the case for me.

From January 1, 2015, to May 27, 2015, I logged over 4,000 miles. I was also working on my master's degree at Liberty University at the time. After much prayer and thoughtful consideration, I decided to take the 2015 spring semester off so I could devote the necessary time to training. Instead of going to seminary, reading, commuting, and doing the assignments, I averaged about fifteen to twenty hours a week cycling. One of the longer weeks consumed about thirty hours of riding time and covered about 250 to 300 miles.

I created a four-month training plan for us. It started with ten hours for the first week and increased two and a half hours every week until it reached thirty hours, tapering until we left. Even though we all set out in hopes of riding every mile of the trip, I could tell during the training rides that it wasn't going to be a reality. We decided it was a team effort, and as a team, we would ride across America. I was blessed with the strength and stamina to ride all the miles, but it was a challenging task, to say the least.

We had our "Biking the USA for Yahweh" mission-team meeting in January 2015. It was a chilly day, but it didn't seem extremely cold. After our meeting, Aaron, Greg, and I decided to go for a little ride. We hoped to ride about twenty miles, cycling around a six-mile loop in Boones Mill. However, we barely completed the loop once because of our cold extremities. The wind hitting our faces was painful and unbearable for longer than just a few miles. Rides like this one were not fun, but they made us mentally tougher.

I strongly dislike cold weather. I'd rather sweat than freeze any day of the week, so I was actually looking forward to cycling in the warm weather of June. Dave, Greg, and I met at our church one evening for a ride. We caught up with Aaron a few miles down the road at the house where he was living at the time. I remember looking at the Weather Channel app earlier and seeing that there was a chance of rain. I sent the guys a text saying, "Rain or shine, we will ride." I knew we needed to ride some in the rain to prepare for the days on the trip that it might rain.

As soon as we left the church, I regretted that I had forgotten my gloves, but we pressed on. By the time we got to Aaron's, which was only three or four miles down the road, my hands were solid red. It was so cold—like a deathly cold. I was really hating life at that moment. Thankfully, Aaron let me borrow some gloves. They were cut-off gloves, but they were much better than nothing at all. We continued on our ride, trying to make the best of the situation.

Just to make things clear, the Weather Channel app forecast called for a temperature in the low 40s with a chance of rain that day. As we were coming to the end of our ride, freezing rain started. Yes—freezing rain. I remember saying, "Way to go, Weather Channel app. I think you messed that one up." Our new sarcastic joke was "The Weather Channel app is never wrong." By the time we got back to the church, my fingers, hands, and feet were completely numb.

I was soaking wet and shivering, I could barely talk, and every part of my body was ice cold. I jolted into the church, went directly into the bathroom, put my hands over the vent, and prayed to God for relief. It was the worst bicycle ride I had ever been on. If I could have, I would have bailed and gotten somebody to pick me up. I'm glad I did not give up, though, because that wintry ride provided me with the mental toughness I would need on some of the rough days of cycling across America.

From that moment on, I decided that if the forecast was for cold weather with the possibility of rain, I wasn't going to ride. I decided to buy an exercise bike and a trainer[2] so I could ride indoors. It wasn't the smartest investment, but you live and learn. Nonetheless, just before

---

[2] A bicycle trainer is a special piece of equipment used to make it possible to ride a bicycle stationary. They are commonly used to train inside during inclement weather or to warm up before a race.

I bought the trainer for my bicycle, I decided to spend some time on the exercise bike. Somehow, someway, I rode for four hours on it. I was drenched in sweat. Every inch of my clothing was completely soaked with perspiration. I looked and felt atrociously disgusting.

Since it got dark early during the winter months, I was forced to either ride the exercise bike or the trainer. I remember doing three-hour trainer sessions in my parents' basement to fulfill my hours of training for the week. Sometimes I'd ride for an hour in the morning and a couple of hours in the evening. To pass the time, I would watch television while cycling. Generally, the television was used as a distraction to lessen the intensity of my ride. I would take it easy during the commercials, but when the show was on, I would increase the power. Those long hours of stationary cycling paid major dividends on the trip. Hard work pays off and is much better than raw talent. Hard work beats talent when talent doesn't work hard.

Aaron, Greg, and I were riding a 33-mile loop from the church one day to train. We found a few spots to rest along the route in order to regroup. We all had experienced our share of physical exhaustion. Some had experienced more than others, but it was my turn this day. Greg and I decided we were going to try to snag some Strava trophies. (If you have the Strava GPS Cycling and Running app, you know how much fun it is.) At the time, Aaron didn't have the special cycling shoes, and that made it challenging for him to hang with us for some of the segments.

Greg and I took off pretty fast. We rotated pulls. It was a blast, but when we pulled into the gas station off Brambleton Road, I began to see little dots. The dots began to get worse, so I decided to walk to an area out of the way. I was staggering around the parking lot like a drunk man in a bar. I came very close to falling, but somehow I managed to hold it together. I leaned over the handlebars to try to find some relief. I almost blacked out. Once I drank some water, the dizziness went away. After a few moments of resting, we jumped back on the bikes to finish the last several miles of the ride.

I guess the warm weather mixed with dehydration took its toll on me. I figured my heart rate would have maxed out since I almost passed out, but I was wrong. I was completely dehydrated. I learned the importance that day of staying hydrated while riding. From that moment forward, I guzzled down many liters of water on every ride. Situations like this one helped prepare me for the heat of June 2015.

My first bicycle club ride was not your typical twenty- or twenty-five-mile jaunt with some grub afterward. It was the most demanding ride I ever rode. It was seventy-three miles with over 9,000 feet of elevation gain, and it was on Good Friday. I guess you could say Good Friday didn't seem so good after a few thousand feet of vert. That day we climbed Peakwood, Mill Mountain, Roanoke Mountain, Naff Road (the wall), Wades Gap, Adney's Gap, Chestnut, and Twelve O'clock Knob. If you know anything about these climbs, then you know they're not the easiest ones to tackle—especially all in the same ride.

The ride started out with a pretty large group of fifteen to twenty people, but the further along we went, the fewer cyclists remained. I was riding really strong up Peakwood, Mill Mountain, and Roanoke Mountain—probably a little too strong. Truthfully, I had no clue what I was getting myself into. I'm sure the other cyclists were saying, "Wow. He's either in really good shape, or he's going to be long gone by the end of the ride." I chuckle to myself when I think about this ride because I was inexperienced on endurance rides that included a lot of climbing.

When we were going up Adney's Gap on Callaway Road, I thought I was going to die. My legs were on fire. They burned so badly after all the grueling climbs that even though I tried to hang with the front group as long as I could, I eventually fell back to the second group. Ultimately, I was the last one to the top. One of the club riders stayed back with me and maintained our conversation to keep me going. I don't remember what we talked about, but I remember it distracted me from the pain I was feeling. After getting to the top, I ate some food and felt a lot better, but we still had two major climbs to go.

I crawled up the steep side of Chestnut Road. That road makes a 10 percent gradient seem flat. On the final climb, I lost sight of the other riders early on. I was just happy to get to the top. A little later we made it back to Patrick Henry High School, where we had begun. The group leader came up to me afterward and offered a word of encouragement. He said it appeared I was ready to ride across America. I felt defeated at the moment, but his words brought victory. Many times during the ride, I almost gave up. The Good Friday ride of 2015 gave me mental and physical preparation to ride across America.

Tuesday and Thursday evenings became times for routine training rides leading up to our big ride. On Tuesdays we rode with the Blue Ridge Cycling Club. I was dropped like a hot potato the first time I rode with them, but the faster-paced rides provided the extra level of training I needed. The Franklin Freewheelers hosted the Thursday Thunder ride, and it quickly became my favorite group ride. From the challenging routes to the friendly people, I loved each moment of training with them. Each of these club rides pushed me to the next level of fitness.

The training rides provided me with the preparation needed to perform very well on the trip. Without all the long days in the saddle, whether on the roads or indoors, I would not have gained the physical, mental, or spiritual stamina and strength needed to endure each mile. Taking the semester off from graduate school and spending countless hours on the bike were some of the best decisions I made to become better equipped to accomplish my goal.

FAILING TO PREPARE IS PREPARING TO FAIL

Cycling across America encompassed its own challenges, but planning the entirety of the trip manifested its own complications. There were some tough moments of preparing for everything, but one of the easiest parts was figuring out how many miles we would ride each day. It was more time consuming than anything. I had to figure out how many miles we could realistically ride each day, along with finding a town where we could stay. There were many towns along the way, but not all of them contained campgrounds, hotels, or places to lodge.

I devised three different game plans for our team to consider and vote on. I wanted everyone's input because I didn't want negative feedback along the way such as "Well, we should have scheduled this" or "We should have scheduled that." The first route plan contained one rest day. The second schedule had two rest days, and the third had three rest days. A rest day was considered a day when we did not ride any miles on the bicycle. A couple of the guys lit up when they saw the three-day rest option, but when they noticed the intensity of the mileage, we were all in agreement to choose the one-day rest option. The three-day rest plan called for some 170-plus mile days.

I was jokingly serious with everyone when I said, "I've gone through the maps several times plotting these plans. If you don't like the choices that have been provided, you're more than welcome to go through the maps yourself and come up with a better option." There were no takers, and everybody agreed with the first route plan. Whenever somebody brought things up during the trip, I reminded them that we all had agreed on it and that they had declined their chance to create a better plan.

It was harder than anticipated when I created those plans. Theoretically, we would average one hundred miles a day. In reality, it wasn't that simple. For example, I could map out one hundred miles, but the only place to stay might have been on the side of the road. Plus, some of the towns were so small that they didn't have a gas station. The maps from the Adventure Cycling Association brought us through a few very large cities, but mainly we would ride through small-town America. It was really cool to see the different atmosphere in each. Experiencing everything from the hustle and bustle of San Diego to the simplicity of the smallest county in Texas was quite an adventure in itself.

Believe it or not, we rarely deviated from our schedule. Here is what it looked like:

Wednesday, May 27, 2015: Depart from Clearbrook Baptist Church at 4:00 p.m.

Sunday, May 31, 2015: Arrive in San Diego, CA

Monday, June 1, 2015: San Diego, CA (Map 1)–El Centro, CA (Map 5) = 121.5 miles

Tuesday, June 2, 2015: El Centro, CA (Map 5)–Blythe, CA (Map 8) = 109.5 miles

Wednesday, June 3, 2015: Blythe, CA (Map 8)–Wickenburg, AZ (Map 13) = 112.5 miles

Thursday, June 4, 2015: Wickenburg, AZ–Apache Junction, AZ (Map 16) = 98.5 miles

Friday, June 5, 2015: Apache Junction, AZ–Safford, AZ (Map 22) = 124 miles

Saturday, June 6, 2015: Safford, AZ–Silver City, NM (Map 26) = 109 miles

Sunday, June 7, 2015: Silver City, NM–Caballo, NM (Map 29) = 73 miles

Monday, June 8, 2015: Caballo, NM–Las Cruces, NM (Map 31) = 74 miles

Tuesday, June 9, 2015: Las Cruces, NM–Fort Hancock, TX (Map 36) = 112.5 miles

Wednesday, June 10, 2015: Fort Hancock, TX–Van Horn, TX (Map 39) = 70 miles

Thursday, June 11, 2015: Van Horn, TX–Alpine, TX (Map 42) = 110 miles

Friday, June 12, 2015: Alpine, TX–Sanderson, TX (Map 46) = 85 miles

Saturday, June 13, 2015: Sanderson, TX–Del Rio, TX (Map 50) = 123 miles

Sunday, June 14, 2015: Rest Day

Monday, June 15, 2015: Del Rio, TX–Leakey, TX (Map 54) = 100 miles

Tuesday, June 16, 2015: Leakey, TX–Fredericksburg, TX (Map 57) = 98.5 miles

Wednesday, June 17, 2015: Fredericksburg, TX–Bastrop, TX (Map 62) = 125 miles

Thursday, June 18, 2015: Bastrop, TX–Richards, TX (Map 66) = 120 miles

Friday, June 19, 2015: Richards, TX–Thicket, TX (Map 69) = 86.5 miles

Saturday, June 20, 2015: Thicket, TX–DeRidder, LA (Map 72) = 116 miles

Sunday, June 21, 2015: DeRidder, LA–Bunkie, LA (Map 76) = 101 miles

Monday, June 22, 2015: Bunkie, LA–Jackson, LA (Map 79) = 97.5 miles

Tuesday, June 23, 2015: Jackson, LA–Poplarville, MS (Map 82) = 126 miles

Wednesday, June 24, 2015: Poplarville, MS–Hurley, MS (Map 86) = 82 miles

Thursday, June 25, 2015: Hurley, MS–Pensacola, FL (Map 89) = 125 miles

Friday, June 26, 2015: Pensacola, FL–DeFuniak Springs, FL (Map 94) = 84 miles

Saturday, June 27, 2015: DeFuniak Springs, FL–Quincy, FL (Map 94) = 103 miles

Sunday, June 28, 2015: Quincy, FL–Madison, FL (Map 100) = 98 miles

Monday, June 29, 2015: Madison, FL–Gainesville, FL (Map 104) = 116 miles

Tuesday, June 30, 2015: Gainesville, FL–St. Augustine, FL (Map 107) = 93 miles

We gave this itinerant schedule to all the members at Clearbrook Baptist Church. It helped them better understand where we were, what we were doing, how many miles we were riding, and how they could pray for us. Due to some inclement weather, our shortest day ended up being about 51 miles, and our longest day was 151 miles.

After we agreed on which itinerary to use, I began to call churches in every city where we were staying. My goal was to schedule a church

Preparation Is King

service of some sort every single day of the trip. I wanted to minister in each town, encourage the churches, and share the gospel. God was in control of everything, and we were able to be involved in many churches along the way. Calling churches was easier said than done. Since I am a Baptist pastor, I wanted to stick with as many Baptist churches as possible, but the vast majority of them wouldn't return my phone calls. Go figure.

When I made the calls to the churches, I would say, "Hey. My name is Bryan Ratliff, and I am the pastor of Clearbrook Baptist Church in Roanoke, Virginia. I'm leading a unique mission trip on a cross-country bicycle ride in June 2015. We will be in your area on [I'd say the date]. Would it be okay if we joined you for worship? We'd be honored to assist you in any way while we're there."

After some discussion, I would direct them to our website, church website, and Facebook page so they would know we were legitimate. I would also tell them our twofold purpose: (1) raising gospel awareness in the USA and (2) raising money for the building fund of Clearbrook Baptist Church.

I always informed the churches that we did not charge anything for our services and that we had already raised the finances for all our expenses. I told them that if they wanted to provide a love offering, it would go toward our building fund. Many of the churches I spoke with were very kind and willing to host us. If some weren't interested, I told them I understood and to have a blessed day. For not having any connections or contacts to schedule meetings, I was amazed at how God opened doors of opportunities for our team to minister.

Mindy, Hannah, Andrea, and Elisabeth devised meal plans. My recommendation was to make a seven-day meal plan and stick with it throughout the trip. I don't think they liked my idea, because they created a fourteen-day meal plan. The food was great. It was nutritious and, for the most part, delicious, but everything tastes good when you're starving. The ladies worked very diligently to make sure four starving cyclists were well fed. Surely one could survive on fast food on a cross-country bicycle trip, but I thought it was in our best interest to eat as healthy as possible. Even though we sometimes didn't eat dinner until around 9:00 p.m., I believe it provided the fuel our bodies needed to complete the physically draining trip.

There was a lot of planning that occurred for this trip. As the saying goes, "Plan your work and work your plan." That's exactly what we did. We devised a training plan and stuck to it. We developed an itinerary and followed it. We created a meal plan and, for the most part, stuck to it. Anything done well has a structured plan. Success doesn't happen by accident, nor does it occur overnight. It is obtained by devising a plan and working the plan. All those who fail to plan will be planning to fail.

The Christian Life Is Not a Sprint; It's a Marathon

Imagine running a marathon every day for a month. Very few people would be willing to attempt such a momentous challenge. Just contemplating the meticulous training runs and demanding time commitments would be enough to discourage most from the start. Most people who run a marathon view it as a "one and done" goal and do not try to run a second one. Riding one hundred miles a day for thirty consecutive days was like running a marathon every day. It required many things, but the main requirement was the discipline of pacing ourselves.

Becoming disciplined enough to know when you can lay down the hammer and when to take it slow is not as easy as you would imagine. On long days, we had to take it slow in the beginning so we'd have the physical strength to finish the ride. When climbing up the long mountains, we learned to take it at a comfortable pace. If we pushed too hard going up, our energy reserves would be running on empty the rest of the ride. Pacing was the key to finishing each day without giving up. I had to learn to use my mind to control my body. My mental strength had to outweigh my physical strength during those moments.

When I think about pacing ourselves on our trip across America, I'm reminded of Ezra in the Old Testament. He was a scribe and a priest who prepared his heart to seek the Lord. Ezra 7:10 says, "For Ezra had prepared his heart to seek the law of the LORD, and to do it, and to teach in Israel statutes and judgments." Ezra provides a wonderful example of preparing our hearts to serve God daily. Are you daily preparing your heart to seek Christ? Christ said that if we seek God first, all our needs will be met (Matthew 6:33).

Prepare yourself spiritually by reading the Word of God. Do you know that about 80 percent of the American population have never read the Bible? Sure, they may have heard a sermon from it or read portions of it, but the majority of Americans have never read the entirety of the Holy Scriptures. What's interesting is that over 70 percent of Americans say that they believe the Bible is inspired by God. How can someone believe in a book they have not read? How can someone reject the contents of a book they have not read?

Perhaps the reason why many Christians are in a spiritual slump is because they are not spending time reading and/or meditating in God's Word. One of the most important things a believer can do is read the Bible every single day. Every time I read it, I learn something new. Perhaps a lot of Christians make the mistake we made on the trip: we were so busy ministering to others that we neglected our personal walk with the Lord. On most days, the only time I spent meditating in the Word was when I read the daily Bible verse from the YouVersion Bible app. That's not the ideal setup, but something is better than nothing. Make time to read God's Word every day, even if it's only a few verses.

Prepare yourself spiritually by spending time in prayer. On our trip, we began every bicycle ride with prayer. We tried to end the day with prayer as well, but unfortunately, we didn't always do that because of how busy we were. Spiritual growth occurs when we take time to talk to God in prayer. It's great praying with a group of people. It's awesome praying with a partner. It's encouraging when others pray for you, but there needs to be a time every single day when you communicate with

God. Prayer is simply talking to God. Take every burden, worry, fear, trial, triumph, victory, setback, and future decision to God in prayer.

If you desire to have a vibrant relationship with God, you need to pace yourself along the way. Years ago, I set a goal of reading the Bible through in a month. I decided to do this while on Christmas break when I wasn't as busy as during college. Everything went well, and I stuck to the plan until I went back to college. You can set a more realistic goal of reading the New Testament through in ninety days. For example, you can read three chapters of the New Testament a day and finish it in three months.

Perhaps you could end the day with a time of prayer before going to bed. It really doesn't matter when you pray. What matters most is that you spend time praying to the Lord. You can do this when you're driving down the road, after you get ready each morning, on your lunch break, when you get home from work, or right before going to bed. I personally use a prayer journal and write out my prayers. It helps me focus and gather my thoughts, and it allows me to bring my requests before the Lord. Spending time with God in prayer will dramatically increase your spiritual growth.

Prepare yourself spiritually by worshiping with a local body of believers. Hebrews 10:25 says, "Not forsaking the assembling of ourselves together, as the manner of some is; but exhorting one another: and so much the more, as ye see the day approaching." Scripture informs us that whenever we abandon the localized body of believers, we are not in God's will. Attending local worship services is not God's suggestion; it's His divine declaration.

For athletes to get better, they have to compete with better players. This principle is true for every sport. If you desire to become a faster cyclist, then you need to ride with cyclists who are faster than you. In like manner, if you desire to grow in your relationship with God, then it's vitally important that you surround yourself with other believers in order to become stronger in the faith. Fellowshipping with believers of like faith will greatly aid in growing closer to Christ.

Obtaining greater knowledge of the Holy Scriptures surely begins with opening the Bible and reading it for yourself, but you'll also greatly benefit by talking to other Christians who are more knowledgeable than you about God's Word. In fact, find a spiritual mentor. I highly recommend utilizing your minister, youth pastor, Sunday school teacher, or small-group leader as a mentor. It certainly wouldn't hurt to use all of them. You can ask questions about what you've been reading, and they can help guide you along the journey.

Once you find a spiritual mentor, try to set aside at least one day a month, preferably two to four times a month, and allow them to invest in you. More is caught than taught. In other words, I learned from my mentors just by watching them serve in ministry. Certainly, I asked them some questions—okay, a lot of questions. I'm sure they got annoyed at times, but I wanted to know more about God's Word. I would spend time reading the Bible with them, praying with them, and ministering with them. I learned more about prayer and ministry just by listening and observing. Do yourself a favor and let a stronger believer coach you for a season.

The Christian life is not a sprint; it's a marathon. Pace yourself along the way. Don't expect to be able to do what seasoned pastors do. They have dedicated their lives to studying God's Word and proclaiming the gospel. Set small goals until you're ready to achieve larger goals. There's no greater feeling than accomplishing a spiritual goal. There is nothing in life more important than your spiritual walk. Take it seriously.

CHAPTER 4
God Is Sovereign

God is absolute and controls all circumstances in the world. He is in control of the planets that orbit the sun, He is in control of all the galaxies in the universe, and He controls every person's life. He is the omniscient, omnipotent, and omnipresent sovereign God. He reigns from His heavenly throne overseeing, orchestrating, and observing all events of all time. It's hard for the finite mind of man to comprehend how the sovereign God of the universe desires to look after His creation, but He does. I want to share some ways that God sovereignly watched over us while we were traveling across America.

∽o∾

GOD IS SOVEREIGN IN HIS PROVISION

God provided every piece of cycling equipment for our team members. When I first started looking into purchasing a nice bicycle, I was shocked at the cost. My mind was blown away at it all. You have to understand that before this escapade, I never owned a bicycle that wasn't from Walmart or Kmart. I first thought that it was just one bike shop overpricing everything to make a quick dollar, but after visiting every local bicycle shop and surfing the internet, I realized that my assumption was wrong. In order to purchase a nice bicycle, I had to lay down some cash.

Since I was going to be riding across America, I was willing to pay for a really nice bicycle. After doing some research, I decided that I wanted a long-distance endurance bike. I found the 2015 Giant Defy Advanced 2 on Giant's website. When I saw it online, I knew it was the bike for me. It had twenty-two gears, disc brakes, and a comfortable setup for riding one hundred miles every day for a month straight. I walked into Cardinal Bicycle, browsed around for a bit, and told the staff what I wanted.

They immediately looked it up online and said, "There's a small chance it may not get here for a couple of months. It'll probably come within two weeks, but it's just a worst-case scenario."

I thought, *Great. Just my luck that the bicycle I want will not get here until the end of 2014.* Literally, the very next week I received a call from the bike shop saying, "Bryan, your bike is ready." I was stoked. I dropped everything I was doing, dashed to Cardinal, purchased the bicycle, and went for a short ride.

My first ride on the nice bike wasn't the best experience. The bike had no shocks, and I felt every little bump. I wasn't used to that. On my first spin, I was expecting to do some lightning bolt speeds compared to all the other bicycles I had ridden, but I didn't really go much faster. Changing the gears was definitely an adjustment as well. I remember asking myself, *Bryan, are you sure you made the best decision in buying this bike?* A few rides later, after getting used to the curved handlebars and all, I realized my transaction was a solid choice.

I'm sure you're curious about how much I paid. You could just google the price, but I'll be nice and satisfy your curiosity. The bike was about $2,000. Aaron Wallace bought a really nice Diamondback bike. His bike was about the same price, or maybe a little more. Dave Schultz bought a nice used Raleigh for just under $1,000, and Greg Parsons got a 1990s vintage Trek for about $400. His bike was such a classic that it made me smile every time I looked at it. The shifters to change gears weren't on the handlebars—they were on the frame. Greg demonstrated that you don't need the newest, most expensive bicycle to ride coast to coast. We all decided to get fitted properly to be as comfortable as possible.

From the bicycle to spare tubes, from tires to chain lube, God provided every piece of equipment for us along the way. There were a few times we had to stop at a local bicycle shop to buy more tubes and such, but all our cycling needs were met. We give God praise for how He provided for us along the way.

God provided opportunities for us to minister in many churches. We were able to schedule seventeen different churches during our exploit. Unfortunately, not all of them came through, but we were blessed by God to be involved in each of the churches we visited during the journey. In some of the churches we just stayed the night, but others allowed us to have a service to share what we were doing. From block parties to gospel sings, we had a blast ministering.

God provided our team with food. It may not have always been our favorite meal, but it was nourishment for our bodies. From the support team preparing our daily meals to the congregations providing the occasional meal, God daily provided our food. We surely had an appetite all day, every day. I'm certain Dave, Greg, Aaron, and I looked like a bunch of pigs when we'd go through the line for fourths and fifths at meals, but we were starving all the time. It didn't matter how much we ate for breakfast, lunch, or dinner, or how many snacks we ate on the saddle, the food never seemed to last us long.

When we were in El Centro, California, we ate some barbecue sandwiches at a local restaurant. While waiting out the rain in Round Top, Texas, we grabbed some food from a local restaurant. We told the waiter about our trip, and he very kindly gave us some free pies. We were amazed by the hospitality we received. We had a great breakfast with Pastor Bob at a wonderful restaurant in Sanderson, Texas. In Arizona, we took a ten-mile detour just to eat some burgers at In-N-Out Burger. As I was eating those juicy burgers, I decided to call my family back home and inform them that I was eating some double cheeseburgers in Phoenix, Arizona. In Del Rio, Texas, the church members took us to an awesome Chinese buffet. A church in DeRidder, Louisiana, provided three wonderful meals for us while we were in their town. In Bunkie, Louisiana, the church folks stayed up past 10:00 p.m. just to make sure we had dinner. In Mobile, Alabama, a lady hosted us for some BLT sandwiches in her home. The food was delicious, and the memories are priceless.

God provided a motor home and trailer for our trip. One team member, Howard, came to me after a worship service and said, "Hey, Bryan. If you provide the fuel cost, I'll drive my motor home for you all." I had a hallelujah shouting moment in my mind when Howard told me that. Perhaps he noticed by the gigantic smile on my face, but I was super pumped about his willingness to serve the Lord. Kevin also agreed to help drive, and these two fellas were a godsend to our team. Without them, we wouldn't have been able to travel like we did. We praised the Lord that God provided a motor home and two drivers for our trip.

God provided a place for us to sleep every night. Whether we stayed in a campground, on a church property, or on the rare occasion in a hotel, God's provision for sleep accommodations was apparent. We may have been a little crowded in the RV, but it was a fun experience for us all. There was only one night when we weren't sure where we would be staying. We were scheduled to stay in a church parking lot in Jackson, Louisiana, but that plan fell through. We drove around parts of Louisiana and Mississippi until after 10:00 p.m. before we found a hotel to crash in. I remember another time when we were driving into a campground late at night. It was extremely run down and not worth staying in. In the midst of not knowing where to sleep, the sovereign hand of God provided for us once again, showing us another place to stay. Our hearts were relieved and grateful for God's provision.

God provided every penny of our expenses for the cycling tour. Leading up to our departure on May 27, 2015, we had several gospel music sing fundraisers and dinners at our church to raise money for our trip. We budgeted about $10,000 for everything. We ended up renting a car to drive from Texas to Florida to make it easier on the ladies doing the grocery shopping. After some adjustments, this unexpected expense not only helped the ladies, but it also allowed the motor home crew to go ahead of us to set up at our next destination. We stayed very close to our budget and were pleased with the outcome.

God provided us with an oil change in Arizona. We were in Wickenburg, Arizona, when Howard and Kevin noticed that the RV needed an oil change. They began to look around online and in some of the other resources they brought. Wickenburg is a beautiful town, but it isn't very big. I would never have imagined there would be a Ford dealership in the town, but there is. We witnessed God's provision in many different ways, especially in providing a dealership with the proper equipment to give the motor home an oil change.

God provided over $30,000 for Clearbrook Baptist Church's building fund through this exciting adventure. Our church was blown away at the response that our daring cycling spree had on people's willingness to join our cause. In 2015, our church launched an official building campaign to raise money for a new building. Leading up to the departure, I encouraged all the church members and faithful attenders to prayerfully consider donating financially. I recommended that they give a certain amount for every mile, such as one cent, five cents, ten cents, twenty-five cents, fifty cents, seventy-five cents, or even a dollar a mile—or any other amount they felt led to give. After everyone contributed, we gave God the glory at the overwhelming response.

Several people in our community donated to us, as did some of the churches where we ministered. I remember someone telling me, "Bryan, I'll donate $1,000, and if you ride every mile, I'll give another $1,000." I contacted the individual after our trip and let him know that we had made it and that I had been blessed with the strength to ride every single mile. A few days later, he came to the church with a check for $2,000. God provided in a big way, and we give Him all the glory, honor, and praise for the outcome.

As I think back upon how God provided for us every step of the trip, I am reminded of Philippians 4:19–20. It says, "But my God shall supply all your need according to his riches in glory by Christ Jesus.

Now unto God and our Father be glory for ever and ever. Amen." If the sovereign God of the universe was able to provide for us in June 2015 while we were pedaling across the United States, then He is able to provide for you too. It doesn't matter what you're going through; God can provide. The will of God will never lead you where the grace of God cannot sustain you.

✌∽o∽✋

God Is Sovereign in His Direction

God directed us to travel along the Southern Tier. There are three standard cross-country cycling routes made by the Adventure Cycling Association. They are the Northern Tier Route, the TransAmerica Trail, and the Southern Tier Route. Both the Northern Tier Route and the esteemed TransAmerica Trail are well beyond 4,000 miles. As much fun as it would have been to do either of them, we decided to do the Southern Tier because it was about 3,000 miles. I purchased maps for each of the routes in order to study them in detail.

Even though the Southern Tier Route took us through the desert during the summer, I believe it was a great choice. Believe it or not, my body adapted well after a few days in the heat. I got to the point where I didn't enjoy being in the air conditioning because it was so cold. Once we made the transition from the dry heat of the desert to the humidity of the Gulf Coast, I felt like I was at home. We seemed to sweat a lot more from the eastern part of Texas through Florida, but training in Virginia trained us to cope with it. I firmly believe God sovereignly guided us to the Southern Tier.

God directed me to Cardinal Bicycle to meet Devin. After browsing around the different bicycle shops and deciding I wanted to purchase a Giant bicycle, my only local option was to go 'to the Cardinal Bicycle shop. Even though all the other bike shops in Roanoke, Virginia, are great, God sovereignly led me to this shop to put Devin in my path. A few years earlier, Devin had cycled across America on the TransAmerica Trail. Since he had pedaled across several states, I knew God was directing my steps.

I sometimes felt like I was pestering him and the others in the shop with all my questions, but Devin always patiently shared words of wisdom and encouragement. It was cool to meet another individual who had done what I was about to do. His purpose hadn't been the same as mine, but he was able to help me prepare for some of the things that might transpire along the way. Hearing his stories was inspiring to me. They helped me anticipate some of the challenges I would encounter along the way. I quickly realized God was directing me each step of the way, even where I purchased my bike.

God directed me to Panera Bread to meet some locals who had ridden across America. I was attending a local preachers' fellowship and asked for prayer for our cross-country bicycle journey. Afterward, one of the pastors told me to contact his friend Maynard. I contacted Maynard, and we met for lunch. He was thoroughly impressed with all the preparation I had done so far. He had ridden across America from San Francisco to Roanoke a couple of years before. Maynard offered some great tips regarding what to do and what to expect. I even went on a few training rides with him. The more locals I met who had cycled across America, the more inspired I became.

Maynard also directed me to a group called Roll Over Cancer. They were the group he had ridden with across America to raise awareness to fight cancer. He said they met once a month at a local restaurant, and he suggested that I attend a meeting to talk with them. Upon his recommendation, I went to Panera Bread one evening and had a great time with them. Several of the fellas who had cycled across America shared their stories, and I listened intently. I asked many questions, to which they graciously responded. They were very kind.

I remember sharing with them my game plan for doing the excursion in thirty days. I appreciated their forwardness when they told me, "Thirty days is a little much. You should consider switching it to forty days." I informed them that I only had the month of June to do this, and I was going to make it happen. I was confident I could do it in thirty days because Pastor Greg Locke had done it in ten days. As I shared that with them, their mouths dropped to the floor. They were flabbergasted that a minister had accomplished such a feat in only ten days.

They offered another piece of advice after looking at our proposed itinerary. The guys said, "You don't want to start off at 120 miles on Day 1. You should consider easing your way into it." As you read earlier, I really wish I would have taken their advice. However, our itinerary included scheduled lodging spots as well as daily mileage allotments to which we wanted to strictly adhere.

Nevertheless, it was a learning experience for me. Perhaps if I had listened to their words of wisdom, we wouldn't have encountered so many difficulties on the first day. I believe God directed me to each of the individuals who had cycled from coast to coast and who taught me. I am beyond grateful for God's sovereign hand guiding me to the right people.

So many times on this trip, God reminded me of Proverbs 3:5–6: "Trust in the LORD with all thine heart; and lean not unto thine own understanding. In all thy ways acknowledge him, and he shall direct thy paths." This verse means so much to me because it reveals the biblical truth that when we put our entire trust in God, He will guide every step of our lives. Sometimes during life experiences, it's easy to think we're just coasting along without any providential guidance, but we can rest assured that God sovereignly directs our steps each day. Throughout our cycling expedition, God gave us crystal-clear direction each and every day.

Where God guides, He provides. Just as God guided and provided for us in June 2015, He can do the same for you in your life. Look to Him for guidance, direction, and wisdom for the future. He will guide you as long as you allow Him to do so. Psalm 37:23 says, "The steps of a good man are ordered by the LORD: and he delighteth in his way." Are the steps of your life being directed by Jesus Christ?

GOD IS SOVEREIGN IN HIS PROTECTION

I was reminded of Psalm 91 time and time again during our excursion. It says,

> He that dwelleth in the secret place of the most High shall abide under the shadow of the Almighty. I will say of the LORD, He is my refuge and my fortress: my God; in him will I trust. Surely he shall deliver thee from the snare of the fowler, and from the noisome pestilence. He shall cover thee with his feathers, and under his wings shalt thou trust: his truth shall be thy shield and buckler. . . . For he shall give his angels charge over thee, to keep thee in all thy ways. (Psalm 91:1–4, 11)

God sovereignly protects His people. Never forget the biblical truth that God will protect you. It doesn't matter what you're going through or what you're facing in life. The Lord Jesus Christ is willing and able to offer protection during your tribulation. There is no mountain too high nor valley too deep that God cannot shelter you under His wings. God loves you and wants to keep you from harm's way. Second Thessalonians 3:3 says, "But the Lord is faithful, who shall stablish you, and keep you from evil." God has established the assuring promise of His faithfulness to guard every Christian from the evil darkness of this world. Look to God for protection when things get tough.

CHAPTER 5

The Trip to San Diego

On Wednesday, May 27, 2015, we met at our church in Roanoke, Virginia, to head out to California. I was truly amazed at all our church family who assembled to send us off. I hardly even had enough time to pack my belongings in the RV or trailer because everyone wanted to talk and take pictures with me. For once in my life, I felt like a celebrity. Church members, family, and friends came out wearing our custom-designed T-shirts. There was much excitement, enthusiasm, and energy that day. It was electric.

While we were greeting everyone, some of the church members generously helped load the RV. With all the luggage we brought, we practically needed a doctorate in organization to fit it all in the trailer. Miraculously, with everyone's help, it got done. I wasn't expecting so much help but was very grateful to them. After we got on the road, it was a little hard finding our belongings since we weren't the ones who had loaded the RV.

One of the greatest lessons I learned from this trip is that we brought way too much stuff. We even brought a grill and stored it in the back of our trailer! I mean, who doesn't travel with a grill? We had the brilliant idea that we would cook steaks, hamburgers, and hot dogs while staying at some of the campgrounds. I thought that was a splendid idea at the time, but we actually never used the grill—not even once. It's kind of funny thinking about it now. There were so many other things we stored in the trailer and never used. We even brought a tandem bicycle that we only used twice.

Our departure day was full of chaos and excitement. *Did I bring everything I needed? I hope I didn't forget anything.* Many other thoughts were racing through my head as well. So many church members, family members, and friends came out to send us off that it distracted me from most of the anxious thoughts. Some folks even brought us a bunch of food, including many cans of tuna. Tuna is one of my favorite meats. I could eat tuna patties all day. They're so good! Think of cooking salmon patties, but replacing the meat with tuna, and you have yourself an awesome meal. When I saw some church members placing a box of tuna cans in our trailer, it made my heart glad.

During the journey, however, my gladness quickly turned into sadness every single time I mentioned it to the meal preparation crew. I remember asking them if they would make some tuna salad, tuna patties, or tuna sandwiches since we had all that tuna. Whenever those ladies didn't want to do something, they'd just look at each other and start smiling. I guess they were telepathically communicating with each other. Literally, that's the way it seemed. After a few moments they would respond, "Bryan, we don't like tuna. We don't like the smell of it. We're not going to make anything with tuna in it." Whenever I tried to rationalize with them that the tuna had been donated for us to use, they would just brush it off. I eventually just gave up and came to the realization that I probably wouldn't be eating any tuna on the trip.

Prior to our adventure across America, we decided that we were going to eat nutritiously. We agreed that in order to function to our greatest potential, we should not pattern our eating habits after those adventure cyclists who consumed the majority of their meals at fast-food chains (like having ten cheeseburgers from McDonalds). It may have worked for them, but we wanted to supply our bodies with nutrients proven to increase energy and boost metabolism. I cannot remember where we were, but I recall Howard asking me how I liked the stuffed peppers. I told him I really liked them, but I could tell by his facial expression that it wasn't his favorite meal. Kevin and Howard gave us a hard time whenever we'd eat turkey bacon. They'd always joke about how it wasn't real bacon.

While scheduling church ministry meetings for our trip, I informed the pastors, secretaries, or whomever I was speaking with that our team members played music and would be willing to minister in that fashion. I personally brought my guitar and harp. Yes, it was a full-size harp with thirty-six strings. It opened up many doors to share the gospel through music and testimonies about the trip along the way, although we didn't really have room for the harp in the RV. It's not exactly the easiest instrument to transport. One of the ladies once accidentally backed into my harp and knocked it over. Her eyes were bigger than mine. I remember picking up the harp, opening the case, and analyzing it. Not even a scratch. It frightened us more than anything.

A couple of days prior to our start on June 1, 2015, we pulled into an RV park in San Diego around 10:00 p.m. It was jam packed, and before we found a spot to park, our driver drove into a dead-end section. As he was backing up, we heard a loud BANG. It sounded as if we had rear-ended another RV. My heart was pounding, and I was very nervous. I was relieved to find out that we had only jackknifed our trailer. Unfortunately, it left a mark, but it was much better than hitting someone else's motor home.

The next day, Kevin made a great suggestion of riding from the beach to the RV park on Sunday, May 31, 2015. Before he made the recommendation, I was telling the team how we'd probably have to leave the motor-home park around four o'clock the next morning to get a good start. We were anticipating a lot of traffic and didn't really know what to expect. Kevin's idea was money in the bank. It was like finding one hundred dollars in one of your pockets. It was an unexpected idea, but a good one. The only regret I have about it is I didn't think of it.

I'll never forget going to the beach in San Diego. I anticipated spending a little bit of time soaking in the beautiful scenery there, but we encountered some unexpected events when we arrived. I loved seeing the greenway along the bay. I loved all the shops, the diversity of people walking around, and the beauty of the Pacific Ocean. It was the first time I had ever seen it, and it was awesome. We found a parking spot, albeit an illegal parking spot. Literally seconds after we parked there, a man walked up to us saying, "You know you can't park there, right?" I remember Howard and Kevin saying, "Yeah, we know. We'll only be a minute." We barely had enough time to unload our bicycles, look around, get set up, and take a picture. Then we were off. Things were a little different in the big city. We weren't in Roanoke anymore. We took a short video and posted an update on Facebook, and then we went for about a twenty-mile warm-up ride back to the RV park. From this experience, I learned that things on the East Coast are much different from things on the West Coast. It was like a different culture.

The first few nights of the trip were an adjustment for us all. It took some time for us to get used to sleeping in the motor home. We all settled into our spots to rest. The most challenging part about sleeping the first few nights was getting used to all the noises. There was the sound of the air conditioner, cars, people outside, and the unexpected snoring. I figured at least somebody would snore on the trip, but I didn't think it would go down the way it did. Some nights the snoring was pretty loud and not pleasing to the ear, especially while we were trying to go to sleep. Perhaps all the adjustments were a factor early on. Once we started cycling, though, I didn't have a problem sleeping or being bothered by the snoring at night because of how exhausted I was.

CHAPTER 6

California: Expect the Unexpected

Without a doubt, life is full of unexpected events. It does not matter if it is family related, job related, or related to a close friend. Every person encounters situations that catch them off guard. Cycling across America with a group of people is no exception to the rule. Trust me—as much planning, scheduling, studying, and analyzing that was required for an endeavor like this, we were bound to miss something. Believe me when I say this: it was almost a daily thing for us. There were many unexpected events that caught us off guard, but we were able to learn some valuable spiritual lessons from them.

NEVER UNDERESTIMATE UNEXPECTED EVENTS

Never underestimate the difficulty of riding a bicycle across America. It is far easier said than done. Whether you're an experienced cyclist or you just bought your first bicycle, it's one of the most challenging tasks anybody could ever set out to accomplish. Very few people ever complete it. I am blessed, privileged, and beyond grateful to have been able to do it, but it came at a cost in terms of the amount of sacrifice, hard work, dedication, devotion, and even faith required to achieve the goal.

Preparation for the trip was vital, but there were some things that occurred that no amount of planning could have anticipated. Just think of someone dumping several barrels full of ice-cold water on you to wake you up. There's not much you can do to prepare yourself for something like that. Similarly, we experienced many unexpected events that were out of our control and for which we could not have prepared.

June 1, 2015, was the first day of the trip for us, but it was also a major wake-up call for me. We left the RV park in San Diego just before sunrise, at around 5:00 a.m. It seemed as if I had woken up every thirty minutes during the night and looked at the clock. My mind was active and wondering about all the different variables we were about to face. My heart was pounding out of excitement to finally get started. I was ready, or so I thought. I woke up before my alarm clock went off, jolted out of bed, woke Dave and Greg, got dressed, drank a liter of water, pumped up my tires, lubed the chain, turned on my lights, and had a time of prayer before leaving the support crew, who were still fast asleep.

I had the biggest grin leaving that RV park. I thought, *Everything is going according to plan. We've got this, and nothing can take this smile off my face.* Little did I know that even though my day was starting in victory, it would end in defeat. For me, the first day was the hardest day of the trip. Keep in mind that I rode every mile of every day, but that was nothing compared to the unexpected difficulties we were about to face on that first day.

We had agreed to schedule a 120-mile ride for the first day. This was *my* brilliant idea, and somehow Dave and Greg agreed. If my memory serves me correctly, Dave attempted to talk me out of it. The maps we purchased from the Adventure Cycling Association were great atlases. They included a lot of helpful information, including the elevation profile of the roads. Somehow, someway, though, I completely blew it by miscalculating our anticipated elevation gain. When I did the calculations, I estimated between three thousand and four thousand feet. In fact, I remember saying, "If we hit four thousand feet, I'd be surprised." Well, we actually climbed over seven thousand feet of elevation gain on Day 1. It may not sound like a big difference, but if you rode your bike up those mountains, you'd understand.

Most of the climbs back home in Roanoke are no more than a couple of miles. There are a few longer ones around, but they're generally not too steep. We rode them all during training rides, but we weren't prepared for the climbs that never seemed to end. None of the climbs in the Roanoke Valley adequately prepared us for the mountains in California on Day 1. The views were great, and that made it worth it, but the elevation gain affected each of us both mentally and physically.

As we were finishing the climbing outside of San Diego, we got to a small town that had an old phone booth right outside an ice cream shop. Some of the team members couldn't resist the ice cream, but I couldn't resist taking a selfie in the photo booth. After getting my selfie, I proceeded to lather up on some sunscreen. I was already feeling a little toasty but thought it would help to put on the sunscreen. I opened up the bottle, and nothing but clear water came out. I thought, *Um, that's some weird-looking sunscreen. I bought it from the health food store. That's probably why it looks different.* I didn't give it much thought until I noticed that it wasn't working—not working at all. It was an epic fail. I thought the health food store had ripped me off, and I was frustrated.

After another pit stop, I gave the bottle a little shake, opened the cap, and white sunscreen came out instead of clear water. All my frustrations were redirected from the health food store to myself. I was as red as a lobster. My skin was on fire. It hurt every time my clothes rubbed it or when I touched it. To top it all off, I was mad at myself because I hadn't shaken the bottle earlier. I learned a great lesson that day: shake the sunscreen bottle before using the sunscreen.

For some portions of the trip we rode on back roads, greenways, and main roads, but in other areas, the maps called for us to ride on the interstate. It is legal is some states to walk, ride, or run on the interstates. Believe it or not, the only way to travel through certain areas of our journey was on the interstate. We began our first major descent on an interstate in California. I didn't look at my speedometer much, for obvious reasons, but I remember glancing at it once and seeing that I was going over 40 mph. For some reason, the speed limit for the traffic was lower than normal, and we were flowing along with the traffic.

At one point, there was no wind because we were riding in the middle of a canyon full of rocks. I'll never forget the name of the canyon. They called it "Devil's Canyon." Strava[3] called one of the segments "Descent into Hell." I guess they named it this because it was so hot at the bottom. As soon as we rode out of the canyons, things opened up, and a very strong crosswind took us by surprise. It blew me several inches from the side of the road into the flow of traffic. That was when Dave and I decided to slow down. Greg continued the pace. He seemed very comfortable, and we caught up with him a few miles later.

Not only were we battling the crosswinds, but we also had to dodge all the rocks on the shoulder. There was everything from small pebbles to rocks as big as a shoe on the side of the highway. It was frightening. Imagine traveling well over 30 mph on a bicycle through a canyon called "Devil's Canyon" and having strong crosswinds catch you by surprise as traffic zoomed by you while you were dodging rocks on the shoulder of an interstate that had a giant cliff drop on your right that contained scores of gigantic rocks! It looked like it went on for miles and miles. That would make an atheist want to be saved! My hands gripped the handlebars so tightly that my knuckles were turning white. When we finally caught up to Greg, we were glad it was all behind us.

The unexpected elevation gains, the long miles, the triple-digit heat, the sunburn, and the exhaustion all combined to get the best of me on Day 1. I was done, and we still had ten or fifteen miles to go before arriving at our destination in El Centro, California. My stomach hurt and I had a severe headache. I told Greg and Dave that I had to stop. I remember walking into the motor home and looking at the support team. I saw defeat in each of their eyes. It was like they were all asking in their minds, *Bryan, are you sure we're going to be able to do*

[3.] Strava is a cycling application for cell phones that records your rides and offers competitive segments along roads to compare your times with other riders. It's a social media app for athletes, specifically cyclists, runners, and triathletes.

this? Day 1 began with much excitement and vigor, but it ended with discouragement, defeat, and lethargy.

While riding a hundred miles on a bicycle, the typical cyclist may burn somewhere between two thousand and four thousand calories, and maybe more, depending on the terrain and intensity level of the ride. As you'd expect, it would be an understatement to say that the cyclist would be hungry after such a ride. However, I was not hungry. I was not hungry at all. All I wanted to do was go to bed, but we had some obligations that evening that prohibited me from going straight to sleep. It would be a few hours before I could lay my head on the pillow.

The pastor and his wife of the church we were staying at were very hospitable to us, and I'm beyond grateful for the generosity they bestowed upon us. After that difficult first-day ride, though, it was difficult for me to enjoy taking a tour of their church, hearing their stories, and even going out to eat with them. Normally I would have eaten four or five barbeque sandwiches, but that day I could barely eat one, and I only ate it out of respect because somebody else was buying my meal. I wasn't hungry at all. I don't remember much about the dinner other than getting a picture with the pastor and his wife and doing everything within my power to stay awake.

I'm ashamed I wasn't better company that evening. After we got back to the church gymnasium, we got set up for bed. Just before going to bed, I lathered some of the aloe oil all over my sunburn. I remember not being able to move on the air mattress because I hurt so much. To my surprise, I woke up the next morning around five o'clock full of energy, hungry, and ready to get back on the bike. I'm sure the aloe oil and a good night's sleep contributed some, but I know without a doubt that God's healing hand upon me gave me strength for the next day.

I distinctly remember one thing the pastor told me. He quoted Galatians 6:9: "And let us not be weary in well doing: for in due season we shall reap, if we faint not." God used that verse to give me strength in the days of much weariness that followed. Unexpected events are going to happen, and sometimes we underestimate things. I greatly underestimated Day 1, but

God intervened and gave my weary soul strength. God can also give you the strength you need to travel through any unexpected circumstance. Trust Him. You will reap in well doing if you do not faint.

Unexpected Events Will Happen Whether You Like It or Not

Whether we like it or not, we cannot escape unexpected events in our lives. They are inevitable. It seemed like every day of our trip was full of surprises, and there was nothing we could do about it. It was out of our control, and we just had to roll with it. Interestingly enough, as I look back at the unplanned circumstances, I believe they made our trip more fun. Imagine living life with everything always going according to plan. That would be boring. When things catch us by surprise, life gets more interesting.

"Bump on your left. Bump on your right. BUMPS EVERYWHERE!" I shouted to Dave and Greg behind me. We were zooming about 30 mph on a two-lane road, making our way to El Centro, California. It was a slight downgrade, probably 1 or 2 percent, and we even had a tailwind. We were having the time of our lives on that stretch! There was no traffic in sight, and we could see for many miles in front of us. Even though the first day had been a great wake-up call for us, we were introduced to some of the bumpiest roads of America that day.

When the potholes started, they were relatively small and few, but they kept getting larger and more frequent. Desperate cyclists do desperate things. Don't judge us for what you're about to read, because if your rump had been on a bicycle with us, you would have done the same thing! We tried avoiding the bumps. They were spaced out and it was kind of fun at first, but the occurrences began to pick up in frequency. In fact, sometimes we had to hop over them. They were massive at times, and it's a miracle we didn't get a flat.

We tried everything to find some smoother pavement. Smooth pavement to a cyclist is like fried chicken to a Baptist! The shoulder of the road didn't work well for us, and neither did our lane. One of us started riding on the white line before going over into the shoulder. It worked some of the time. We tried both white lines. Remember, I said not to judge us. There was no traffic and we could see for miles each way, so we didn't see the harm in riding on the wrong side of the road. But in the end, even that didn't work. It was still too bumpy.

Then we found the sweet spot. It was the yellow lines in the middle of the road. Looking to our right, we could see the main interstate and the border of Mexico. If we looked to our left, we could see some mountains in the distance. All we could see in front of us and behind us were miles and miles of flat land. The sun was beaming down on us. It was hot, but we found smooth pavement. We were pretty stoked about that.

After several miles of cruising on the yellow lines, our sweet spot disappeared. The bumps were completely unavoidable. All we could do was pedal a few strokes and stand up to avoid the discomfort of all the bumps. We didn't really see any smoother pavement until we got into Louisiana. Don't get me wrong—we had some smooth stretches, but we hadn't expected to travel on America's bumpiest roads.

The road bumps we encountered on the trip were similar to the bumps we face in life. It doesn't matter if you're driving down the interstate or cycling down a back road; sooner or later we all are going to hit a pothole. Sometimes the best thing we can do when we ride into the potholes of life is to just keep going. Sure, it may slow us down or cause some problems, but we just need to keep moving forward. The bumps we face in life can be annoying, but I believe God uses them to help conform us more to the image of Christ.

Each of the unexpected events we faced brought its own set of challenges. It's funny that there was nothing we could have done to prepare for them. I believe God can use unexpected challenges in life to draw us closer to Him. Bring on the unknown and be conformed more to the image of Jesus Christ.

Embrace Unexpected Events

Embracing unexpected events allows us the opportunity to grow in ways we never could have imagined. One of the biblical characteristics God expects out of pastors is hospitality (1 Timothy 3:2). While riding across America, I did not expect to learn this biblical truth in each church where we were privileged to minister.

After the first few days of cycling, I was sound asleep in the bunk above the driver's seat when a severe pain hit me. I had muscle cramps in both my calves. I tried to roll over, but it just made it worse. The cramps extended up to my hamstrings. Talk about real pain. Cramps all over both my legs while I was in the bunk wasn't an enjoyable experience. Did I mention it happened in the middle of the night? The pain was so intense that I felt like screaming at the top of my lungs. I couldn't, though, because I would have awakened everyone. So I stretched out as far as I could in the bunk bed, opened my mouth wide, and screamed as loud as I could in my head.

Whenever you ride one hundred miles a day for thirty days, you can expect pain—everywhere. You will have pain in places you wouldn't even imagine, like in your fingernails and toenails. Okay, not really that extreme, but you get the idea. I remember sitting in the motor home while the muscles in my calves and thighs would just twitch. It didn't hurt, but it was somewhat entertaining to watch.

I never anticipated the amount of pain all the mileage was going to cause. The greater the mileage, the greater amount of pain. It is the same in our lives. The longer we live, the more pain we will experience. Every person who walks on God's green earth is going to experience it to some degree. However, it's not about how much pain we experience, but it's about how we use the pain to advance the gospel. Our greatest pains can become God's instruments to help save lives.

Romans 8:28 says, "And we know that all things work together for good to them that love God, to them who are the called according to his purpose." I believe that everything happens in life for a specific purpose and plan, both for our good and for God's glory. Are you willing to let God use your painful past for His perfect plan? God can turn every tragedy into a triumph by the power of the gospel of Christ. Embrace the unexpected events, whether past, present, or future.

We encountered many unexpected events on our journey across the United States. The best thing we did was embrace them with open arms. A willingness to embrace circumstances that arise in our lives allows us the opportunity to experience life's greatest moments. The same goes for the Christian. God allows unexpected events to arise in our lives so we can grow in our faith. Embrace unplanned situations because doing so will help you become a better follower of Christ.

PREPARE FOR UNEXPECTED EVENTS

Preparing for unexpected events seems rather pointless since it's pretty much impossible to know what to plan for, but it's essential to expect circumstances to arise that were not anticipated. None of our team members, riders, or support crew members had ever done anything to this magnitude before. We all knew things would arise that none of us were ready for, and we did try to prepare ourselves mentally for such occurrences.

Have you ever been so hungry that an entire meal barely made a dent in the surface of your hunger cravings? The average human being burns around two thousand calories a day. Generally speaking, the average person has to consume approximately two thousand calories to maintain the same weight. We anticipated burning between two thousand and four thousand calories daily on our trip. Some of our training rides had produced similar outcomes, but during training we weren't cycling one hundred miles day after day. To say it mildly, we never seemed to have enough food.

Cycling across America is the greatest weight-loss program any person could embark upon because you can eat whatever you want, as much as you want, and still lose weight. It's almost unfathomable until you do it. When I started training, I weighed about 145 pounds. When I weighed myself after getting home, I was 130 pounds soaking wet. To say we were always hungry is a huge understatement. I prepared myself for this, but the preparation was not enough. I didn't expect to be as hungry as I was, and it was the same for the other cyclists.

When the extreme hunger urges came, I remember my hands shaking because I needed some food. I'll never forget the first time this happened. It was June 3, 2015, our third day riding, and we were in the town of Blythe, California. We could see the state of Arizona just beyond the campground where we were staying. We were cycling through the downtown region of Blythe. It seemed like every traffic light was red. We stopped and started too many times to count, but at one of the stoplights, someone shouted from their car, "Hey! We saw you guys on the interstate outside of San Diego." I thought that was super rad. I wish we'd had time to talk with them more, but we didn't.

As soon as they drove off, the hunger hit me like a ton of bricks. My pockets were empty, and I was starving. It was the providence of God that we were only a few miles away from the campground. When Greg and I got to the campsite, I devoured everything I could get my hands on. From that moment forward, I was *always* hungry. I could never get full. I remember eating a large meal in the motor home, hopping back on my bike for a few miles, snacking on the food bars in my back pocket, sipping some water, eating some energy bars, and doing it all over again.

My go-to sandwich was almond butter and honey. Sometimes I'd even throw a banana on it. Yes, I have a sweet tooth, and it hit the spot, as they say. I never got sick of those sandwiches, and I ate a couple of them almost every day. In fact, I still eat them regularly. I'd say I consumed around four thousand to five thousand calories every day. We knew exactly how much to eat and drink each hour, but most of the time our bodies needed much, much more than our estimated calculations.

Those who know me know that I don't like to drink extremely cold water. I drink room temperature water without flavoring. It only took two or three days baking in the desert sun for that to change. After that, I wanted my bottles completely full of ice, and I desperately needed flavoring. On the trip, plain water became disgusting to my taste buds. I'm not sure why; maybe the plastic taste was getting into the water. That seems logical to me, but all I know is plain water made me gag. Even though we planned to drink lots of water and eat a ton of food, we did not anticipate the amount of food we'd actually eat and the volume of liquids we would drink.

All our training miles paid off during the trip. While training, I was never concerned about becoming another Lance Armstrong, but I was focused on logging miles and putting time in the saddle. It helped me prepare physically, emotionally, and spiritually. I did not expect the severe saddle sores, though. I'll try to be as discreet as possible, but every morning I lathered my backside with a special ointment. I also invested in cycling shorts with a cushion so my bottom would be more comfortable. One thing I should have invested in was a better seat. Oh well. Lesson learned for the next cycling adventure. The shorts and ointment helped, but there's only so much they can do when you're on a bicycle eight hours a day.

Make no mistake—no amount of preparation can fully prepare you for riding a bicycle across America. Just when you think you've done all you can to be prepared, you discover that you did not prepare enough. This reminds me of the Christian life. There's nothing we can do to plan for or prevent unexpected circumstances from happening. God has a way of helping us get through them, and the experience draws us closer to Himself. Continue preparing for the future, realizing that it is called *the unknown* for a purpose. God doesn't want us to know what lies ahead because He wants us to trust Him with our future. Are you trusting God with your future? Proverbs 3:5–6 says,

"Trust in the LORD with all thine heart; and lean not unto thine own understanding. In all thy ways acknowledge him, and he shall direct thy paths."

BE WILLING TO LEARN FROM UNEXPECTED EVENTS

The greatest thing we can do when unexpected events occur is to learn from them. I believe unplanned situations that come up in our lives are the best form of education. While traveling across the United States, I learned the most valuable lessons from events that were never planned. I learned many great lessons on our trip, including shaking a sunscreen bottle, applying aloe oil, properly reading the elevation profiles on our maps, eating the appropriate amount of food, and drinking a whole lot of water. If you are not willing to learn from what happens in your life, you are missing out on one of the greatest forms of wisdom.

Those who are not willing to learn are not willing to experience growth. Imagine moving away from home, going to college, investing money in an education, and not taking the courses seriously. It would be complete foolishness to attend class with headphones on, watch YouTube during class, surf the internet, never pay attention to the professor's lectures, or never read the assignments. Talk about a waste of time and money! In like manner, we make the same mistake when we choose not to learn from the unexpected events that transpire during the course of our lives. It matters not if the circumstances are good or bad, for we can learn something from them all.

Devote the rest of your life to being willing to learn from everything that life brings to you. Whenever life brings you ups or downs, commit yourself to gaining wisdom from what takes place. Being a disciple of Christ literally means being a learning follower of His teachings. From the Sermon on the Mount to the Pauline Epistles to the book of Revelation, Christ has valuable lessons for each Christian to glean when they take His Word seriously.

Throughout each of these unique, unexpected events, God taught me different lessons. One of the best lessons I learned on this trip is the truth of this profound thought: You never know what life will bring. In fact, even after I completed this endeavor, God continued to teach this to me. I've learned more about the brevity of life and the reality of death. I've learned that the consequences of sin can affect all those around you, but the cure for sin is found in a personal relationship with Jesus Christ.

I want to take this opportunity to encourage you not to avoid unplanned moments in your life. Embrace them. Learn from them. God has a special lesson in each event of life. Trust God in the times for which you are not prepared. James 4:13–14 says, "Go to now, ye that say, To day or tomorrow we will go into such a city, and continue there a year, and buy and sell, and get gain: Whereas ye know not what shall be on the morrow. For what is your life? It is even a vapour, that appeareth for a little time, and then vanisheth away."

CHAPTER 7

Arizona: Journeying through the Desert

Ifelt like Moses leading the Israelites through the wilderness when cycling through Arizona—at a much smaller scale, of course. The wilderness Moses led the Hebrews through was dry, desolate, and a desert. Arizona had its own form of beauty, and I appreciate the beauty of God's creation in the desert areas of the state. While riding my bicycle through this uniquely beautiful area of the United States, I learned three valuable spiritual lessons.

ENTERTAINING ANGELS UNAWARES

Day 3 was an exhilarating day as we embarked upon more of the roads of Arizona. Dave, Greg, and I zipped along at a steady pace, anticipating a mountain that was off in the distance. We had no idea what type of climb that would be because the maps were not always the best precautions; they did, though, inform us about the few miles of climbing. It was an overcast day, with the sun periodically popping out of the clouds. The weather seemed great that day compared to some of the heat we experienced on the first couple of days.

When we were riding, we always observed the road signs to better prepare for the unknown road conditions ahead. My heart pounded with excitement and vigor every time I saw a road sign warning of an upcoming descent. As we were cycling along, a sign telling of a downhill 7 percent gradient over the next few miles seemed to pop up out of nowhere. Instantly I shouted, "GREG! This is our chance to set that high-speed personal best!" Prior to leaving, I set a personal goal of hitting a certain speed, and this was the chance to do it.

I looked behind me to see if any traffic was coming up. It was clear, so we took off. I got out of the saddle, laid down the power, and began the descent. We positioned ourselves in an aerodynamic way to gain as much speed as possible. I got behind Greg to catch his draft. I glanced at the speedometer, and it read 35 mph. Then it read 45 mph. I looked one last time, and it said about 52 mph. Once I crossed my goal of going over 50 mph, I rose up out of the aerodynamic position so the wind would gradually slow me down.

As we reached the bottom of the descent, I shouted, "WOOOOO! OH YEAH!" The adrenaline that was flowing through my veins was uncontrollable. We were whooping, hollering, shouting, smiling, and laughing all at once with great excitement. What a rush it was! We were on cloud nine, stoked about our speed. When I looked back from the bottom of the descent, I saw that we had left the motor home in the dust! That was cool. Looking back at it all, perhaps it wasn't the wisest or safest decision to go that fast. Oh well; it was fun!

Needless to say, we talked about that accomplishment for the next several miles until we came across another cyclist riding in the opposite direction. We hadn't seen another cyclist on the road since the beach in San Diego. We shouted, "Hey! What's up?" and waved. A couple of minutes later he turned around and rode with us for a few miles. I had heard about people riding across America who met other cyclists along the way. In fact, I heard about one man and woman who met while touring and later got married. I wasn't anticipating anything like that, but I was excited about the possibility of meeting fellow cyclists.

It was really cool how he just stopped what he was doing, turned around, and rode with us for a couple of miles. I don't remember too much about our conversation, but I remember we told him what we were doing and gave him a tract. He told us about a girl who was cycling across America solo with saddlebags. He told us a little about her and her cause for pedaling from coast to coast. She was a few days ahead of us, but I thought it would be cool if we caught up to her. The cyclist gave us a heads-up about the climb we were to tackle a few miles ahead. We were very grateful to have met him, and we were glad to have embraced the moment.

The interesting part about this encounter was how randomly this guy popped up on the road. We didn't see him coming to begin with, and he disappeared in a matter of seconds. None of us even remember his name. It was somewhat bizarre. The more I reflect upon our encounter, the more possible it seems that he could have been an angel. Call me crazy, but the supernatural is real. The Scriptures make it clear that there are angelic beings—not just in heaven, but also on the earth.

It was an angel that guided Moses during the exodus from the bondage of the Egyptians. It was an angel that stopped the mouths of the lions when Daniel was thrown into the lion's den. It was the angel of God that Jacob wrestled, as recorded in Genesis 32:22–32. It was an angel that informed Mary and Joseph about the coming birth of the Messiah. It was an angel that told the shepherds the good tidings of Christ's birth. It was an angel that comforted Jesus Christ in the garden of Gethsemane, and two angels guarded the empty tomb. It was an angel that freed Peter from prison.

Hebrews 13:2 says, "Be not forgetful to entertain strangers: for thereby some have entertained angels unawares." One of the greatest examples of the truth of this verse is found in Genesis 18. Abraham was introduced to three unexpected visitors in the middle of the day. These three men were not ordinary visitors but were God's messengers bearing special news for Abraham. Abraham welcomed these guests warmly and had Sarah prepare them a meal. While preparing the meal, Sarah overheard their conversation about the promise of their future son, Isaac. Their disbelief eventually turned into belief when Isaac was born.

There's no way I can prove to you that the gentleman in Arizona was an angelic being, but I do know he was a messenger sent to us by

God. His message was to inform us of the upcoming climb full of steep gradients, switchbacks, and out-of-this-world views. The word *angel* simply means "messenger." God often sends us messengers throughout our lives, and it's our responsibility to be hospitable when we meet them. Be careful how you treat strangers, because they could potentially be messengers of God.

God Is Our Source of Strength

Dave, Greg, and I were riding in Arizona. To be exact, we were just entering the suburbs of Phoenix. Our support team had stayed in Wickenburg for an oil change. We came to a good-size intersection, and the stoplight was red. Some cyclists really slow down at stoplights so they won't have to completely stop. Dave is one of those cyclists. He doesn't like to stop because he doesn't want to have to unclip his shoes from the pedals. There were two lanes on our side of the road in addition to a right turning lane. Greg and I came to a stop and unclipped our shoes, while Dave was crawling like a snail. I looked away to see if the light had changed, and I heard a little crash. Dave had fallen over. He wasn't hurt; he was just mad. I looked back and saw him slapping the ground out of frustration. After Dave got up and the light turned green, we decided to pull over into the CVS parking lot and take a break. It's always funny when someone falls over—unless you're the one hitting the ground.

There were a few moments on the trip when fear was my greatest emotion, and the day I am about to tell you about was one of them. Fear can sometimes be our greatest enemy and the toughest battle we face in life, but with God's help, it can be overcome. We left Safford, Arizona, one morning en route to our next destination. Dave, Greg, and I started the day together, but there was a stretch when I was riding alone. I remember beginning a climb that lasted a couple of miles. It was a very narrow two-lane road with a huge cliff to my right. The cliff in and of itself did not scare me, but all the tractor-trailers zooming by and buffeting me with their draft made my anxiety level increase dramatically. I could have been blown off the road and over the cliff!

They would lay on their horns while barely missing me. Every time they flew by me, the impact of the wind they caused (their draft) made me swerve to the side of the road and nearly slam into the guardrail. I came close to going off the pavement a few times. I should also mention that there was not a shoulder to the right of the road. The only thing separating me from riding off the cliff into a bunch of rocks was an altogether-too-short guardrail. With all of this going on, I began chanting Philippians 4:13 to myself: "I can do all things through Christ which strengtheneth me. I can do all things through Christ which strengtheneth me. I can do all things through Christ which strengtheneth me."

After riding a little way up a narrow road on the side of the mountain, I noticed a tunnel. As soon as I entered the tunnel, the sound of the tractor-trailers' engines was magnified greatly. It sounded like a war zone with the engines revving up, the horns blowing, the brakes squeaking, and the sound of the creaking tunnel. Perhaps it was my mind playing tricks on me due to the anxiety level increasing, but it seemed like each time a tractor-trailer would pass me, the tunnel would shake. It sounded like it was going to collapse. It was more than a little nerve-racking, but I just kept pedaling one stroke at a time, chanting, "I can do all things through Christ which strengtheneth me. I can do all things through Christ which strengtheneth me. I can do all things through Christ which strengtheneth me."

Arizona brought a unique set of challenges to our crew. Please understand that our team resided in the state of Virginia, where the humidity level makes 80 degrees feel like 95 degrees. While cycling through Arizona, there was no humidity at all. It was in the upper 90s, but it didn't feel like it because there was no humidity. It was a deceptive heat. I experienced two specific results from the dry heat of Arizona: dry mouth and little perspiration.

There were times in the middle of Arizona when my mouth was so dry that I had no saliva to swallow. It was the strangest phenomenon. I had never undergone that before. As you could imagine, I was extremely thirsty at times. I was so thirsty that I felt I could have drunk all the water from an entire swimming pool. I was reminded of what the psalmist said in Psalm 42:1: "As the hart panteth after the water brooks, so panteth my soul after thee, O God." In the same way that I desired water in my times of severe thirst, Christians should thirst after God. Far too often we are guilty of thirsting after the things in this world rather than thirsting after the God who made the world.

Remember, God was Elijah's source of strength when he faced the 450 prophets of Baal. God was Noah's source of strength when he built the ark while facing opposition from all those around him. God was Joseph's source of strength when his brothers sold him to Midianite merchants as a slave. God was David's source of strength when he defeated Goliath. God was Samson's source of strength when he broke down the pillars against the Philistines. God was Sarah's source of strength when she gave birth to Isaac late in life. God was Rahab's source of strength as she guided the Hebrew spies in the land of Jericho. God was Joshua's source of strength when he was marching around the walls of Jericho seven days in a row. God was Hannah's source of strength when she was barren. God was Esther's source of strength when she stood up for the Jewish people before the king. God was Moses's source of strength when he led the Israelites out of Egypt.

God was Peter's source of strength when he preached on the day of Pentecost. God was Paul's source of strength when he traveled the world proclaiming the good news of the gospel. God was Stephen's source of strength when he preached his final sermon. God was John's source of strength when he wrote about the future apocalypse. God was the disciples' source of strength when they committed their lives to following Christ. God was the early church's strength when they were persecuted for advancing the gospel. God the Father was God the Son's source of strength when He died on Calvary for our sins.

It matters not what you are facing in life; God is the greatest source of strength. If God gave each of these biblical characters a portion of His divine omnipotent strength, then He can provide you with the same dose of mighty power. God granted me the physical, mental, and spiritual stamina and strength needed to persevere through this section of our journey. Look to God for strength because He alone is the source of our strength. Keep moving forward. Keep pressing onward. Keep striving upward in faith—believing, trusting, and expecting God to provide you with the capability to journey through whatever life throws at you. With God's divine, sovereign aid, you've got this!

SEEK GODLY COUNSEL

In addition to cycling across America, my eyes were fixed on another goal: cycling across America without a flat tire. How cool would that be? I thought it would make for an awesome story to be able to ride three thousand miles on a bicycle without experiencing a flat tire. My hopes were dramatically crushed on Day 3 when I got a flat tire. I was pretty let down about this because I had bought special Armadillo-brand tires. I had been given that counsel about the tires from a local cyclist in my hometown who had told me about someone who had cycled across America without a flat tire.

Perhaps the person who had made it across America without a flat tire didn't sojourn through the desert in the middle of the summer heat. Imagine how hot the pavement gets in that kind of heat. Perhaps the guy who rode cross-country without a flat using those Armadillo tires didn't have glass, nails, and all other sorts of debris on the shoulders. Considering all that, it is no wonder I got the flat tire. So much for the great advice from the fellas at the bike shop, but there's no way to guarantee a tire won't go flat. However, their sales pitch hooked me and I bought four of those tires just in case I encountered some mechanical issues.

In the middle of Arizona, I noticed that my back tire was deflating. I decided I would ride a few miles, stop, pump up the tire, and start riding again. I repeated this process for several miles until I finally came to my senses and decided to replace the tube. I had been determined not to change the tube in the tire, but after a few times of stopping to put air in the tire, I thought, *Who cares? I'm just going to change the tube.* I pulled off to the side of the road and went to work changing the tube. I caught back up with the crew, and we continued to the next town.

Sometimes we set wonderful goals that should be pursued, but other times the goals are pointless. This was a pointless goal. There is no purpose in riding across America without a flat tire other than being prideful of the fact that it was done. As I reflect upon all of this, I am reminded of the importance of listening to godly counsel in our Christian walk. Just as the guys at the different local bike shops gave me advice for my trip, God's Word presents detailed advice for living out the Christian life.

The phrase about safety being found in a multitude of counsellors is found three times in the book of Proverbs. Proverbs 11:14 says, "Where no counsel is, the people fall: but in the multitude of counsellors there is safety."[4] It is important to place the emphasis where God places the emphasis. The Holy Spirit, through Solomon, stresses the importance of seeking out godly counsel. It was a great idea for me to seek out counsel from experienced cyclists, but it's an even greater idea for believers to pursue spiritual advice from God's Word and from seasoned soldiers of the cross.

A great example of receiving counsel is observed in the life of Rehoboam in 1 Kings 12. Solomon, Rehoboam's father, was credited for placing a large workload upon the Israelites. After Solomon died, Jeroboam, along with the rest of the Hebrews, requested a lighter load of labor. The older men's counsel was the better choice because the Jewish people would have admired, respected, and trusted Rehoboam

---

[4.] Proverbs 15:22: "Without counsel purposes are disappointed: but in the multitude of counsellors they are established." Proverbs 24:6: "For by wise counsel thou shalt make thy war: and in multitude of counsellors there is safety."

for making that decision. They would have followed him and would have done whatever he requested. However, after meeting with some younger men with whom he had grown up, Rehoboam decided to increase the amount of work for the people of God.

More than likely, your situation will never be like Rehoboam's. Most people will not lead an entire nation, but it is certain you will be faced with life-altering decisions. In every decision we make, it's important that we honor God, His Word, and His will during the process. There were times when I listened to and followed the counsel of experienced cyclists. The times I listened, I was grateful, but when I neglected to follow their advice, I regretted it. You will never regret pursuing and following God's will in your decision making.

There will be times when all you need to do is receive the counsel given in God's Word. The psalmist said, "Thy testimonies also are my delight and my counsellors" (Psalm 119:24). God's Word alone contains the information you need during your decision making. There may be other times when you could use advice from a spiritual mentor or pastor. I'm not saying that pastors know more about the Bible than anyone else, but they have devoted their lives to studying the Word and sharing the Word. In many cases, they know more about the Holy Scriptures than the average person in the pew. They might know some specific passages of Scripture that may greatly assist you in your time of decision making. Plus, there is no better person to have specifically praying for you than your minister. In every decision, seek godly counsel.

CHAPTER 8

New Mexico: Climbing Mountains for Christ

While completing our ride through Arizona, we came to a pretty intense mountain full of switchbacks and cliffs around each corner. I was riding solo up this climb and took my time. There was no rush to get to the top, so I embraced the moment. As I pedaled each stroke, I told myself, *Great job, Bryan. That's one more pedal down. You got this.* As I approached the top, I saw Howard sitting on the side of the road filming me with our camera. That brought a smile to my face. He was cheering me on! Everyone else was admiring the beautiful scenery of God's creation. I got off my bicycle and joined the crew for a few minutes to embrace the moment.

I took a short break before the descent down the backside of the mountain. Remember, after every ascent, there is always a descent. For every uphill, there is always a downhill. This is a promise we banked on. While zooming down the roads with some sharp curves, I began to pull away from the motor home. I reached the bottom and crossed into New Mexico. I briefly glanced behind me and saw that the support team had caught up. Once we transitioned from Arizona to New Mexico, the atmosphere instantly changed. It went from desert to mountainous forest where elk roam.

From the moment I entered New Mexico, I fell in love with the unique beauty of the state. The rolling hills were full of open green pastures that you'd see in the movies. I kept my eye out for wildlife but didn't see any. The weather was absolutely perfect. We were on top of a mountain, the skies were clear and blue, and the temperature was around 80 degrees. It was by far my favorite state. I also learned some important lessons about the Christian life in this state. Each mountain we climb in life can be done for the glory of God.

CLIMBING MOUNTAINS REQUIRES GOD'S HELP

Saturday, June 6, 2015, brought our team to a campground in Silver City, New Mexico. After I got settled, I contacted the pastor of the Baptist church in the area where our team would be serving the following day. It had been another one-hundred-mile-plus day, and I was exhausted. My body was beginning to get adjusted to the intensity of the trip, but it still wiped me out at times. We got cleaned up, ate a wonderful meal prepared by the ladies, reviewed what we would be doing in the services the next morning, and then went to bed.

The next morning, we arrived at the First Baptist Church of Silver City around nine o'clock to set everything up. Pastor Jason welcomed us as soon as we got there. We divided our team into two groups for Sunday school. The church gave us a few minutes in each class to share what our trip was all about. I believe that intimate time of fellowship helped the church better understand the purpose of our adventure. In all the hustle and bustle of the morning, I forgot to get my harp out of the RV. About ten minutes before the morning worship service began, Pastor Jason asked me, "Didn't you say you were bringing a harp? I told the church you were going to play it today." I bolted out of the sanctuary, wiggled my way through the motor home, squeezed the harp out, and tuned it up with seconds to spare. Pastor Jason requested that I begin the service by playing a couple of hymns on the harp.

During the worship service, our team members introduced themselves and explained their roles on the team. David, Andrea, Hannah, Elisabeth, and I sang a couple of songs before Dave preached. The title of his sermon was "The Ride of Your Life." In his sermon, Dave shared how he personally had underestimated the difficulty of the trip. Truth be told, all of us did that. He related it to the Christian life and how God is calling us to ride this life for Jesus Christ. Acts 20:24 says, "But none of these things move me, neither count I my life dear unto myself, so that I might finish my course with joy, and the ministry, which I have received of the Lord Jesus, to testify the gospel of the grace of God."

When I think back about cycling one hundred miles a day and then engaging in services, I wonder how we even did it. There's no doubt in my mind that God helped us pedal every mile and minister in each congregation. No matter the situation, the season of life, or the circumstance, God is able to help. Whether it's a trial, triumph, or tragedy, God can give divine aid. He can give you help when you feel helpless. He can provide assistance when your life is full of turbulence. Each mountain you face is an opportunity to seek God's helping grace! No matter how low the valley or how high the mountain, God is waiting for you to ask Him for His help.

We had a wonderful time worshiping with the people of Silver City, but we had to keep pressing forward. I was in the mood for some chicken nuggets, so our team made a pit stop at a fast-food restaurant. I recall my left rib cage tightening up as I was sitting in the restaurant. I did my best to hide the pain, and I made sure the team members didn't notice. I'm no doctor, but I thought I was having some heart trouble. My mind instantly began thinking the worst possible scenario. *What if I'm having a heart attack?* Thankfully, I was wrong. Dead wrong. It was simply a muscle spasm in the lung region of my torso. This happened a few times on the trip. Perhaps those muscles were being worked too hard and didn't have the appropriate time to rest.

After that brief personal scare, I regained my mental and physical composure, and we set out on about a seventy-mile ride to the small town of Caballo, New Mexico. Dave, Greg, and I had some mental stability issues at the beginning of this day because we planned to crest our highest point on the ride, Emory Pass, and we didn't really know what to expect. We were very intimidated by the 8,200-foot mountain. *Will it be extremely steep? Will there be a bunch of switchbacks? Will the mountain be gruelingly long?* Our minds were racing while our legs were pedaling.

We were not even out of Silver City yet, and out of nowhere a cyclist appeared, riding in the opposite direction. His name was Christian, and he was a local. At first I thought he might have been another angel that God sent us. It didn't take us long to realize he was not an angelic being, but I believe he was still a messenger God sent to us to ease our minds and help us prepare for the climb that awaited. God's providential hand was at work.

Ironically, although his name was Christian, he was not a Christian. He was a very intelligent man, though, who was working as a geologist in the region. In fact, there were mountains with a lot of sediment layers surrounding us. It was almost like cycling through a miniature Grand Canyon. We eventually transitioned the conversation to spiritual matters and shared what we were doing and why we were doing it. We gave a clear presentation of the gospel. He told us that his religion was his bike and his faith was his training. I believe God sovereignly placed us on his path to deliver the gospel message to him. Since we were cycling across America, it was relatable to him, and he listened intently to our presentation. I also gave him one of our pamphlets.

Not only did God prepare Christian to inform us about Emory Pass, but God prepared us to inform him about the good news of Jesus Christ. We were able to present the gospel of Christ to this man while we cycled together for several miles. It was well received, but Christian's words will forever echo in my mind: "My religion is cycling." In other words, he ascribed worth to physical fitness. Did you know that you could cycle across America dozens of times and even win the Tour de France, but if you died and went to hell, there would be no point to those human accomplishments? Jesus said in Mark 8:36, "For what shall it profit a man, if he shall gain the whole world, and lose his own soul?"

If Christ is not your identity, then you will live a life of vanity. If your identity is found in physical fitness, then you've wasted your life. If your identity is found in building wealth, then you've wasted your life. If your identity is found in climbing the corporate ladder, then you've wasted your life. Solomon was a man who once had his identity in God, but his focus transitioned to wisdom, wealth, women, and wine. As a result, Ecclesiastes 2:17 informs us that he hated life. Ironically, it matters not if your name is Christian or if you grew up in a Christian family. In order to be a Christian, you must be born again (John 3:3).

After several miles of cycling with Christian, we began our last downhill together before parting ways. I think Greg really enjoyed his company because on each descent, they left Dave and me in the dust. We thanked Christian for riding with us and for giving us a pep talk about the climb. We said our goodbyes and pressed on. Meeting him was not a coincidence; it was God's providence. It was a divine appointment that God orchestrated from the start.

Some days of our trip were much more challenging than others, but my goal was to successfully ride one day at a time. Some days I was really in tune with the bike, and it was effortless, but other days it was so difficult that I felt like quitting and throwing my bicycle over a cliff. The largest mountain we climbed was Emory Pass. Its elevation was about 8,200 feet. That's more than double the elevation of any mountain I had ever climbed before. I had three goals on this trip pertaining to the bike: my daily goal was to complete each ride, my second goal was to cycle to the top of Emory Pass, and my third goal was to ride from coast to coast.

Armed with what we had learned from Christian, we began our climb. Dave rode as far as he could and told Greg and me, "The mountain is all yours." He rejoined us at the top for the major descent. The difficulty of going up Emory Pass wasn't as bad as we had anticipated. We weren't going for any records. We just took our time going up. There were still twenty-three days left, and we knew the importance of not overexerting ourselves physically. While traveling up, we stopped a few times to take in the beautiful scenery.

At one point, it was like an enchanted forest from the *Hobbit* movies. I was in awe of every tree, flower, animal, and everything else my eyes beheld. The pine trees were the most beautiful trees I had ever seen. They were breathtaking. I remember telling Greg how awesome it would have been for us to stay in one of the campgrounds we passed.

The only drawback was they were only usable with tents, and we didn't have the time or the equipment for such an enjoyable stay. Even though Emory Pass was a large ascent, it would go up a ways and then down some before the final ascent took us to the top of the mountain. I remember going up a short distance and then descending a small hill, hooking around a sharp curve and seeing a section of massive boulders. We looked at each other and agreed it was picture worthy.

The short, punchy climbs mixed with small descents, the sharp curves opening to a view of large boulders, the enchanted forest, the switchbacks, the long, drawn-out climbs, and the breathtaking views overlooking the beauty of God's creation in New Mexico made the climb worth it. When we got to the top of the mountain, you would have thought we had arrived in St. Augustine, Florida. The exhilarating experience of completing the short-term goal of climbing Emory Pass produced excitement, accomplishment, and blessedness. Emory Pass became my favorite part of the entire trip.

Sometimes we get so consumed with the climbs we're facing in life that we forget about the beautiful scenery around us. Whenever we travel through these times, it helps to contemplate what God is doing around us. I realize Emory Pass is nothing compared to Mt. Everest, but it was the largest mountain on the Southern Tier. Riding to the top helped me understand that every climb we face is an opportunity for either success or failure. Use each mountain you face in life as a stepping-stone to success. The day I climbed Emory Pass, I felt like I could overcome any future obstacle. Perhaps you're climbing up an Emory Pass in your life as you read this book. Whatever it is, I assure you that it can be overcome with God's help.

CLIMBING MOUNTAINS MAKES YOU APPRECIATE THE VIEWS
We had just finished ascending Emory Pass, the longest climb

on our trip. It was an unforgettable experience. From the surreal mountaintop views to the wind howling through the air, it was by far my favorite part of the expedition. At that moment, I knew I was going to ride every mile of the trip. I paused to express my gratitude to the Lord for allowing me to achieve this second goal. I prayed something like this: *God, thank You for giving me the strength and stamina to make it to the top of Emory Pass.*

First Thessalonians 5:18 says, "In every thing give thanks: for this is the will of God in Christ Jesus concerning you." Did you know it is God's will for believers to be thankful? The phrase "In every thing give thanks" provides the idea of living a lifestyle of worship through thankfulness. The verse could be paraphrased as "It is God's will for every child of God to live a lifestyle of gratitude." When we are full of gratitude, our faith will soar in altitude! The reason why so many Christ followers are not soaring in their walk with God could be because they are not living lives full of gratitude. When Christians are not living lives of gratitude, they are living outside the will of God. It is far better to be in God's will than in God's way.

Psalm 100:4 says, "Enter into his gates with thanksgiving, and into his courts with praise: be thankful unto him, and bless his name." Being thankful is not God's suggestion; it's His divine declaration! God does not request that His children be grateful, but He expects them to be grateful. When we are not thanking God for what He has done for us, then we are being disobedient to His commandment. Incomplete obedience is complete disobedience. There is something special about expressing your gratitude to the Lord for all He's done. Our team was beyond thankful for the blessings God poured out on us at the peak of Emory Pass. Perhaps you can begin today to thank God for the mountains in your life. Remember, the views after the climb make you grateful for the climb. If we never experience the struggle of the climb in our lives, then we will never be able to enjoy the beauty at the top of the climb. The views are worth the climb!

If you could have been with us at the peak of Emory Pass, you might have thought our team was already on the beach at our destination in St. Augustine, Florida. Joy filled each of our hearts to the fullest! I remember setting my bicycle against the RV, walking over to the elevation sign, and shouting at the top of my lungs, "WOOOO!" My shriek of joy echoed for miles. I waited a few seconds and did it again: "WOOOO!" The smile on my face was as large as the mountain I was standing on! There was nothing anyone could have done or said that would have wiped the smile off my face. Howard, Kevin, Dave, Greg, David, Andrea, Hannah, Elisabeth, and I were rejoicing with all our hearts!

It seemed as if time had stopped at the top of the mountain. There was a little breeze that swayed the limbs of the trees. The clouds blocking the sun made the weather perfect after our long, winding climb. There was not another vehicle or person in sight. The mountain was ours for those brief moments, and I savored each moment. The support team made it to the top a lot sooner than Greg and I did. After we calmed down from the excitement, some of the team members said that there was a little trail across the road with an incredible view. I said, "Let's go check it out. We have time." We crossed the road and set foot on a clear, smooth, narrow path. It wasn't even five minutes before my eyes met with the clouds in the sky. The trees at the top were pretty big, and they blocked most of the view. You could tell it was overcast because the sun wasn't visible, but we didn't have a clear view until we were standing at the end of the short trail.

I was reminded of what Paul said in Philippians 4:4: "Rejoice in the Lord always: and again I say, Rejoice." First Thessalonians 5:16 says, "Rejoice evermore." The word *rejoice* literally means "to be full of cheer." The term *evermore* gives the idea of "always and at all times." Here's how I like to summarize these two verses: "Always and at all times be full of cheer for what God has done for you." Trust me when I say that I did not need someone to remind me to be full of cheer when I was overlooking the sky at the top of the mountain. However, when I was in the process of pedaling up the climb, I needed the reminder. Isn't that how life is? When we are battling the uphill part, we forget the importance of rejoicing, but as soon as we crest the top and begin going downhill, we are full of cheer. Let this scene of our trip be a reminder for us to adopt a spirit of rejoicing in all seasons of our journey through life: as we climb, at the top of the mountain, and during our descent. The views after the climb have a way of making you full of joy!

After a short break of taking it all in, Dave, Greg, and I began our descent. I knew that Greg would be going faster than us since he was very good at riding downhill from mountaintops. He had great bike-handling skills, such as those needed on roads with sharp curves. It was almost as if the road became a part of him and he knew every inch of it, even though he had never ridden on it before. I decided I was going to try to stay with him as long as I could. Greg did not waste any time after leaving the RV. I did my best to keep up with him, but after the first switchback, I fell behind. I said to myself, *Forget it. I'm just going to take my time.* I knew there was no way I was going to keep up with him. Perhaps I could have kept up if I had been more familiar with the descent. I glanced behind me and saw that Dave was right there. I was glad he was there because we got to enjoy the descent together. Dave and I cruised together while Greg glided away into the distance.

When we hooked around the first few switchbacks, the view opened up and we could see for miles. It was as if our ride, at that moment, was in slow motion. Viewing the insanely large cliff just beyond the guardrails and seeing the awe-inspiring manifestation of God's handiwork in creation was a spiritual experience. It has been said that everything is spiritual. I became a believer in that statement that day. I was amazed at what I was seeing. I remember saying, "Wow." It was such an awesome moment. I could find no words to express the magnificence of it all. I just kept repeating, "Wow." We could occasionally see Greg in the distance, but after the first few switchbacks, he seemed to have disappeared. He was long gone and had to wait ten or fifteen minutes for us at the bottom. When Dave and I finally caught up with Greg, we regrouped and were on cloud nine again! We recalled the details of our journey to and from Emory Pass as we cycled to our next destination.

After all that had transpired on Emory Pass, I was, and still am, humbled that God allowed me the opportunity to be part of such an amazing mission and to cycle up that big mountain. James 4:6 says, "But he giveth more grace. Wherefore he saith, God resisteth the proud, but giveth grace unto the humble." It's only by the grace of God that our team made it over Emory Pass. We gave and continue to give God the glory for what He did and continues to do in our lives.

James 4:10 adds, "Humble yourselves in the sight of the Lord, and he shall lift you up." Humility pleases God Almighty. Whenever we accomplish tasks in life, we can either have a humble spirit or a prideful spirit. God hates pride, but He loves humility. No matter what life brings your way, remember to always stay humble. It's not what you have done or what you have accomplished, but it's what God has done and what God has accomplished through you. Never forget that. The views after the mountain make us humble before God because they show us how big God is and how small we are.

CLIMBING MOUNTAINS MAKES YOU STRONGER

As I was growing up, my family would often visit my grandparents. It was not just something we did for Thanksgiving or Christmas, for my parents thought it was important to spend time with them more frequently than that. When I got older, there have been times when I would go visit my grandparents for a week or two as a result of the habit my parents instilled in me. When you spend time with people, you learn their habits, routines, and schedule. My grandparents eat dinner around 4:30 p.m., watch the news at 5:00 p.m., and watch *The Andy Griffith Show* at 5:30 p.m. Each meal is way better than fast food or a restaurant! No matter what is set before me, I know it's going to be delicious. My grandparents have seen all the episodes of the *Andy Griffith Show* more times than I can imagine, and they always get a good laugh out of what Barney Fife is going to do. I must admit that I enjoyed it too! It was good, clean humor.

I'll never forget traveling through the small town of Hatch, New Mexico. The town has fewer than 1,700 people. It's very close to Las Cruces. We were approaching an intersection and had to make a left turn at the stop sign. I looked both ways. There was a white truck coming in the distance, and I remember telling Greg and Dave, "We can make it. Let's roll through the stop sign." Technically this is illegal, but we did it frequently during training and never had an issue. Well, we beat the white truck and pressed on. Soon after that, we heard some sirens, like those from an ambulance or police car. We thought they were just trying to get around us, but the police officer actually pulled us over. Not every cyclist can say they've been pulled over by the police!

We stopped on the side of the road, and I thought, *Can he even give us a ticket?* He got out of his truck, marched over to us like a drill sergeant, and said, "Guys, you have to obey all the laws just like vehicles, which includes stopping at stop signs. You need to ride as close to the shoulder as possible."

I said, "Sorry, officer. It won't happen again." We thanked the officer for doing his job, and we parted ways. We would joke about it throughout the rest of the trip, and we made sure that we came to a complete stop at traffic signs and traffic lights. I guess every town has its own version of Barney Fife patrolling the streets to keep everyone safe.

New Mexico introduced us to many things, but the most interesting was cattle guards in the road. Cattle guards are metal grids covering a ditch that allows vehicles and pedestrians to pass over, but not cattle or animals. The animals would get their hooves stuck between the metal beams if they tried to cross the cattle guards. These things were everywhere. We were cycling in one section of New Mexico that was apparently farm country, because cattle were on both sides of the road. I was riding behind Dave and Greg as we were cycling down a flat stretch of pavement. We saw a herd of cattle in the road up ahead. As we got closer to them, I noticed that one of them was a bull. The horns were massive. I looked behind and on the opposite side of the road to see if any traffic was coming. It was clear, so I took off, putting the pedal to the metal. I gained some serious momentum and crossed over the yellow lines to avoid the bull and the cattle. I thought, *I just need to go faster than Greg or Dave.* I guess our experiences with dogs during training rides made me paranoid that the bull was going to chase us. We all took off as fast as we could and zoomed by the cattle. We looked back and saw them still grazing on the grass on the side of the road. Thankfully, they didn't chase us! All that climbing had made us stronger; we were able to lay down some serious power!

"GREG! GREG! THIS IS OUR TURN!" I shouted at the top of my lungs, but Greg didn't hear me. I quickly tried calling and texting him that we had missed our turn, but he was focused on drafting behind a tractor-trailer. While traveling to Las Cruces, we decided to experiment with drafting for the first time, but not with the RV. It was with a tractor-trailer. The roads were completely flat, we were at a stop light, and it was our opportunity to give it a shot. Greg and I took off and stayed behind the tractor-trailer for a few miles. When I looked back, I couldn't see Dave. We were behind the truck and were going about 30 or 35 mph. After Greg zoomed off in the distance drafting behind the truck, I pulled over and waited for Dave. It didn't take too long before I saw him pedaling along in the distance. I brought him up to speed about missing our turn while drafting and that Greg didn't hear me. We just waited for Greg at the intersection, and it was about fifteen minutes before he realized what had happened and rejoined us.

We were scheduled to conduct a block party at East Mesa Baptist Church in Las Cruces at 5:30 p.m. that day. We were on schedule and took our time after the drafting incident. Dave and Greg made a short pit stop and eventually caught up to me a few miles down the road. We made it to the church in the afternoon and got cleaned up and prepared for all the children. There were at least fifty people there, and we had an incredible time hanging out with the children and teenagers. We ate dinner, played outside on the blow-up slides, and then went inside for some songs and Dave's gospel illusion show.

David always helped us out with music on the trip. He was willing to sing specials and help lead the children in songs. Just before Dave did all his tricks, we sang some songs. I got my guitar out, and we sang all our favorites, including "The Lord's Army." The song goes like this:

> I may never march in the infantry [march in place],
> Ride in the cavalry [pretend you're riding a horse],
> Shoot the artillery [clap hands together].
> I may never zoom o'er the enemy [spread arms out and
> pretend to be a plane],
> But I'm in the Lord's Army [salute and say, "Yes, sir!"].
> I'm in the Lord's Army (Yes, sir!),
> I'm in the Lord's Army (Yes, sir!),
> I may never march in the infantry,
> Ride in the cavalry,
> Shoot the artillery.
> I may never zoom o'er the enemy,
> But I'm in the Lord's Army (Yes, sir!).

Then David did the superhero version:

> I may never fly like Superman,
> Climb like Spiderman,
> Swim like Aquaman.
> Indiana Jones is not the kind of man I am,
> But I'm in the Lord's Army (Yes, sir!).

Both the children and the adults absolutely loved it! Dave presented his magic tricks, and as always, they were a huge hit. We give God praise for giving us the physical and spiritual strength to ride seventy-five miles and then minister to the people of East Mesa.

Some of my team members said, "Hey, Bryan! Are you ready to do this?" I don't remember how, when, or why I agreed to it, but I did. Trust me—when I was reminded of it after the block party was over, I was having major reservations about my agreement. I had agreed to let some of my team members wax my legs. When I first bought my road bike, I told myself, *I'll never wear those tight spandex shorts, and I'll never shave my legs.*

Never say never, right? I was about to eat my words. There we were, gathered in one of the church restrooms. Hannah, Andrea, Elisabeth, David, and Greg seemed to be having way too much fun with all of this. They had their phones and cameras out ready to document and record it all. I remember thinking, *This is a mistake, and I'm going to regret this.*

One of the ladies pulled out a waxing strip and placed it on my hairy legs. I said, "Hold up! Let me put a sock in my mouth." I gritted my teeth, anticipating much pain. One of the girls ripped the waxing strip off my leg. I took the sock out of my mouth and said, "That's it? It wasn't that bad."

Man, I should have never said that! I could see the change in their eyes and in their faces. They were out to get me, and wow—they got me good! I thought, *How bad can it get? I mean, that barely hurt.* All five of them decided to grab their own strip. They each found a place on my hairy legs and then ripped the waxing strips off all at the same time. "AHHH!" I shouted at the top of my lungs like a little girl. Without hesitation, the room erupted with laughter. Some of them were laughing so hard they began crying!

I guess you could say that all the climbing we did leading up to that moment made me stronger not just physically, but also mentally. If I survived my legs being waxed, then I know, with God's help, I can survive anything. Seriously though, isn't that how God works in our Christian lives? He uses each climb we encounter to make our faith stronger. Climb every mountain of life for the glory of God!

Almost all the cyclists I met before this trip shaved their legs. Apparently this makes you somewhat more aerodynamic and able to cycle slightly faster over a long period, but it's mainly done in case there is an accident. Cyclists claim it's easier to clean up flesh wounds on the legs when they're shaved. I really didn't like the idea of shaving my legs. I wasn't really interested in the idea a bit, although wondering whether or not it would influence my speed did intrigue me. Shaved legs did feel a little cooler out in the heat, so that made me happy. However, I doubt that I'll ever do that again. Eh, it's just not for me.

CHAPTER 9

Texas: Laughter Is Medicine for the Soul

Dave, Greg, and I were riding together. The roads were very open. We had not seen any traffic for miles, so we were hogging the road, you could say. We were riding beside each other, fellowshipping and having a great time. We looked behind us, and there were no vehicles in sight. There were no cars in front of us. Greg was on my right and Dave was on my left. I remember that Dave was riding on the yellow line and crossing over at times into the other lane. Out of nowhere, we heard a loud, obnoxious horn honk. It sounded like a honk of frustration because we were hogging the road. We all jumped because it startled us. Dave swerved some and got back on our side of the road. Truthfully, I was a little scared to look at the vehicle passing us because I was afraid they'd be giving us that obscene finger gesture. As the vehicle passed, we saw Howard and Kevin in the RV laughing hysterically at us. It was a good prank, but it certainly scared us.

While cycling along the Southern Tier, we had some serious conversations, moments of cutting up, and periods of complete solitude. It was odd. We'd chat for two hours straight and then go another two hours without saying a word. We talked about theology, philosophy, music, life, the future, girls—anything and everything. Nearly every day we said, "Actually, Dave." Imagine saying this in the tone of a professor who thinks he knows it all. To any conversation that needed some sort of correction, that phrase was added. It was added with such an emphasis that it was probably annoying to the support team. It didn't bother us, though, because we thought it was hysterical.

Whenever someone would say something like "Well, actually, it might be better . . ." or "Actually, this is what it means . . ." we'd obnoxiously say, "Actually, Dave." It may not have been funny to anyone else, but it amused us while we were cycling coast to coast. We brought Aaron up to speed when he arrived in Texas. It became a daily conversation starter, and it made the rest of the team shake their heads, smile, and chuckle.

Whenever I think about our epic journey, it brings a smile to my face. Certainly there are bad times and some ugly times along with the many good times, but it all brings joy to my heart. The Holy Scriptures speak of laughter. From Sarah laughing at the news of bearing a child in her old age to the joy of the Philippian church, God has much to say about laughter. I'd like to take you on a brief journey and share some stories from our adventure across America that make me smile, laugh, and just shake my head. Ecclesiastes 3:4 says there's "a time to weep, and a time to laugh." God can use laughter to brighten our day and bring joy into our lives.

∾o∿

STORIES THAT MAKE ME SMILE

Consuming four thousand to six thousand calories a day and still losing weight is hard to fathom, but that is exactly what we experienced. I've always been a skinny guy, but when I look at our photos, I always say, "Man, I was skinny!" There were random moments when the hunger would hit us, and there was nothing we could do but find the closest thing to eat.

One time Kevin was sleeping on the couch in the living room of the RV, and he woke up around two o'clock in the morning and witnessed Aaron eating a bowl of cereal on the top bunk above the captain's seat. Kevin still gets a good laugh telling that story, and it always brings a smile to my face.

Texas: Laughter Is Medicine for the Soul

It was challenging when we transitioned from New Mexico to Texas. By transitioning, I mean that our team was grooving with a routine, but then it was time for Hannah and Andrea to leave. The routine was solid, and we all were adjusted to it. When Mindy and Aaron met up with us, we went through some minor adjustments in everything from sleeping arrangements to where groceries were stored in the RV, but they seemed major at the time. One day Mindy and Elisabeth were out somewhere in the rental car, probably out shopping, when we stopped for a break to eat a snack in the motor home. I said to Kevin, Howard, and David, "Hey. Where's the bread? I'm trying to make a sandwich."

They responded, "Sorry, Bryan. We have no idea." Fortunately, it only took a few minutes to find the almond butter, honey, and bread, but it seemed like I had to open every cabinet in the RV just to find that loaf of bread. I made my sandwiches, and they were as good as ever. It took a day or two of adjusting, but we managed to do it very well. As I think back on these memories, it makes me smile.

Mindy is a pharmacist at our local hospital and is the closest person we had to a medical doctor on the trip. When she was around us, I always seemed to feel healthier. She had spoken with a registered dietician and was very instrumental in finding out how many carbohydrates we needed to consume and how much water we needed to drink each hour.

Before the trip, we agreed to allow her to ask us these specific questions: "Are you drinking enough water?" and "Are you eating enough food?" When I was drinking enough water and eating enough food, I didn't mind her asking, but when I wasn't doing what I was supposed to, her questions bugged me. I wanted her to do this, but I also told her before the trip that I wouldn't always appreciate it, even though we needed her to do it. She did a great job, though, even when we weren't very easy to deal with. This memory always brings a smile to my face.

Early in the trip, we established the ritual of buying smoothies at the gas stations where we made pit stops. I'm pretty confident that I bought one in every state we traveled through. I'm sure I purchased them in some of the states we traveled through on the way out to San Diego as well. It got to the point that I took pictures of the smoothies I purchased. There were usually only two or three flavors available in gas stations. The green, berry, and strawberry and banana flavors were available in most stores, and whenever another flavor was available, I almost always tried it. I really enjoyed the protein-flavored ones because they contained over four hundred calories per bottle. When I see smoothies now, I am reminded of all the times I drank them across America. It always brings a smile to my face.

Every time I see cowboy boots or a cowboy hat now, it reminds me of our cycling trip from coast to coast. Howard wanted to buy some boots and hats in Texas. I guess everything is not only bigger in Texas, but it is also better. When we arrived in El Paso, Howard managed to find the perfect store. I'm not sure exactly how many pairs of boots and how many hats he bought that day and throughout the trip, but it was enough to make us all smile. His enthusiasm about buying something he wanted brought joy to my heart and a smile to my face. Howard often wears those boots to worship services now, and we reminisce about him buying them out west.

In El Paso, Greg and I saw a Chick-fil-A and could not resist stopping to grab some grub. We got a nice afternoon snack before heading to the motor home for a brief break. When we walked into the RV, everybody said, "I want some too." David, Hannah, and Andrea took food orders for the rest of the team and headed out to buy some chicken sandwiches. Just before exiting the RV, they asked us if we wanted anything else. Greg said, "Yeah, get me one too." Not long after, they departed to get the food, and we took off on the bikes. We made a pit stop later in the day. I remember Greg opening the fridge. He looked around for a few moments and asked, "Where's my sandwich?"

Andrea and Hannah's faces were priceless. They paused, looked at each other, and said, "We forgot. Sorry about that." I could see the frustration on Greg's face. It was as if steam was rolling out of his nostrils and ears in bitter anger. To not get a sandwich you were promised was rough. It was a serious trial and tribulation! I had bought an extra chicken-salad sandwich and told Greg he could eat it. This incident brought Greg, Dave, Aaron, and me some great moments of laughter later in the trip. Our inside joke became "Hey, bro! Where's my sandwich?"

There were definitely times during our trip when smiling wasn't something we could do. Dave's unexpected health concerns was one of those events. He experienced some challenges with his health during the first half of our trip. He recalls how it happened:

> After a seventy-mile ride, I was very tired. David and I were moving a picnic table. I thought it was too heavy, but David said, "It's not heavy," so I walked over and picked it up. When I set it down, I felt a sharp pain. In the service on Wednesday night, the pastor's wife said I might have a hernia. She offered to take me to the doctor. The doctor said I didn't have a hernia, but I needed to rest for several days because I had two strained tendons. After a couple of days of rest in the RV, I decided to ride half the distance each day for five days and then ride the entire distance the remainder of the trip. After returning home, my doctor diagnosed me with a double hernia.

Dave and I even had a hard conversation about the possibility of him going home due to the injury. Thankfully, it never came to that. As we look back at this challenging time of our journey, I smile because God is the Great Physician who gave Dave strength, stamina, and perseverance when he needed it the most!

Several days later we found ourselves in the middle of Texas headed for a small town called Sanderson. The views of the mountainous terrain in that region were out of this world! I'd been told Texas was flatland full of desert. There are certainly some areas like that, but other regions are breathtakingly gorgeous with trees, mountains, and jaw-dropping overlooks.

Just before we arrived in Sanderson, I experienced the same sharp pain in my left knee that I had experienced in my right knee days earlier. I proceeded to do exactly what I had done before with the other leg. I unclipped my left foot from the pedal and pedaled using only my right leg. Luckily, I only had to do this for a short distance until we arrived at our destination. The next day, along with every day following, I had no knee pain. Even though it wasn't something I had anticipated, I'm glad it didn't turn out to be anything serious.

I've always watched the Weather Channel with suspense as the storm chasers were hunting tornados. I remember thinking when I was younger, *I'd like to see a tornado, but from a distance.* After we arrived in Sanderson, Texas, Pastor Bob told us that there might not be many people in attendance for that evening's dinner and gospel sing because there was a tornado warning. As I looked up to the darkened skies and felt the strong wind hit me in the face, I regretted my childhood wish of seeing a tornado. The dinner was delicious, and the gospel sing went well. I thank God that our evening was tornado-free. I have no idea what I would have done if a tornado had hit Sanderson that day. I remember texting a friend about it who lived in Texas, and she helped calm my nerves. Thinking about this always brings a smile to my face.

After the dinner and gospel sing in Sanderson, as we were driving back to the spot where we were staying, a jar of honey slid off the counter and slammed my front derailleur.[5] The derailleur was pretty badly bent, which leads to my next story. Our bike ride from Sanderson to Del Rio, Texas, was 120 miles. We kept hearing a rubber sound on my bicycle. It was an irritating noise, so we decided to stop and check it out. Thankfully, Greg knew what he was doing, and he adjusted the front derailleur so that it only rubbed in the lowest gear. Even though it still didn't work like normal, it operated much better after the adjustment.

I am not a mechanic. I can change the oil and tires on my car, but

---

[5.] Derailluer: a bicycle mechanism that moves the chain out and up, allowing it to shift to different cogs.

that's about it. I enjoy cruising around town in my car, but I've never had an interest in working on one. The same goes for my bicycle. Whenever I'd go to a bike shop, I'd tell them what I was setting out to do and ask them for advice. One of the guys at a bike shop recommended that I become familiar with how to work on the bicycle. He said I didn't have to become a bike mechanic, but it would be a good idea to learn the basics. I'm certainly no expert, but I can change the tires and tubes comfortably. Other than that, I am a fish out of water. I remember being told that if I don't know much about working on bikes, I should be sure that someone on my team does.

Compared to my limited knowledge, Greg was an expert. I'll never forget our rest day. We were at a church in Del Rio, Texas. Greg disassembled every part of his bike, cleaned it spick and span, and put it all back together. I'm sure I could get my bike all apart, but there's no way I'd be able to put it back together. Whenever we were riding in the middle of the desert, in the humid heat, or on top of a mountain, it was great having Greg there to help us through any mechanical problems. This brings a huge smile to my face every time I think about it.

STORIES THAT MAKE ME LAUGH

On Saturday, June 13, 2015, we adventured out of Sanderson, Texas, and rode 120 miles to Del Rio, Texas. The first several miles were a cyclist's paradise. We were in the middle of the desert, and it was overcast and misting. The mist felt great. I remember telling Greg, "Let's try to ride as many miles as we can before it stops misting and the sun comes out." Well, we got about forty miles in, and it felt like the devil had come out to play. It was like a headwind from hell. Yes, I believe headwinds are of the devil. Okay, not really, but it felt like torture the rest of the day.

I remember taking a selfie with the sun in the background. I looked rugged, and I posted the picture on Facebook. The picture shares how the devil was working overtime on us that day with the wind. Eighty miles in a headwind was complete torture. I know it wasn't hell, nor does it compare to eternal separation from God, but it was absolutely horrendous. In my opinion, Day 13 was the second hardest day of the trip. I didn't have a power meter at the time.[6] I wish I did because it would have greatly assisted in pacing. Some parts of our ride that day were on level ground, but it was all we could do to go 12 mph. When I arrived at the Baptist church in Del Rio, I was ready to part ways with my bike.

Arriving in Del Rio was quite an experience. Don't judge me, but when I was extremely tired or needed to make up some time, I would draft behind the motor home. After battling it out with the headwind for over seventy miles, I needed a way to get rid of it, so I decided to draft behind the motor home. I rode behind the RV for a few miles until I saw a border patrol officer zoom past me to stop the RV. I remember saying to myself, *Oh great. I've messed up now and caused Howard to get a ticket for allowing me to draft behind him.* This, however, was not the case. There was a really long bridge ahead, almost two miles long to be exact, and the officer wanted to escort me across. I felt like a celebrity. I got behind the officer and cruised along on the level bridge, but I was completely exhausted from all the headwinds during the day. Through this unexpected event, I learned that people still show kindness. A stranger demonstrated it to me, and it inspired me to do the same. I always get a good laugh whenever I tell this story.

Del Rio was the only town where we had a day to rest. It's really hard to fathom how taxing it was on our bodies to cycle about one hundred miles each day. I remember finishing out the day after dark. It was probably around nine thirty or ten at night when I arrived in the church parking lot. The sovereignty of God was manifested when we scheduled this stop. Pastor Larry and the members of the First Baptist

6. A power meter is a device fitted to a bike that measures the power output of the rider. Most commonly, power meters use strain gauges that deflect slightly when a force is applied. By measuring this torque and combining it with angular velocity, power (measured in watts) can be calculated.

Church were very hospitable. They allowed us to sleep in their facilities. Rest is a vital part of cycling. Perhaps we should have had more than one rest day, but our intense schedule did not allow it. I guess if I ever plan another cross-country cycling adventure, I'll be sure to include more rest days.

We were involved in the morning service on Sunday, and since we slept in the church's lodging quarters, we were able to sleep in a little bit. We attended Sunday school, briefly presented our ministry during the morning service, and helped out with their junior church. After the worship service, the church members took us to a Chinese buffet, which was amazing. I cannot remember how much I ate, but I know I ate a lot!

On a previous day on our trip, we had been so close to Mexico that I was able to snap a photo of a sign that said you were entering Mexico. Nevertheless, I noticed on our maps that Del Rio was very close to the Mexican border, and it was our best window of opportunity to visit, since we had a rest day there. While eating lunch with everyone, I began to inquire about going to Mexico. It was only about ten minutes down the road. Of all the things I could have forgotten to pack, I had forgotten my passport. Some people said I could go across the border without it, but others said I could not. A couple of church members, who were also missionaries, graciously agreed to take me. For some reason, I couldn't convince any of the other team members to go with us. I guess they didn't want to get stuck across the border.

Well, I got in the van with the Young family, and off we went. We didn't stay long, but I could easily tell we were not in America anymore. It was certainly no resort for vacationing, but I was super ecstatic about visiting Mexico. I had always wanted to go there. Everything was so different even though America was just across the other side of the Rio Grande River. The road signs were in kilometers and the roads were not very smooth. By the way, I'm glad we didn't have to cycle across Mexico, because those roads were much rougher than any road we cycled on. The houses were made differently than the ones in the States. More people were walking around than in America. I guess not everybody had the luxury of owning a car. It was also interesting to note that my cell phone signal completely died as soon as I crossed over the river, but it came alive again once we were back in the United States.

A tornado had recently struck the area and had left numerous structures in ruins. It was eye opening to see, especially since it was only about five miles from the church where we were staying. We could see that houses had been destroyed, businesses had been demolished, and families had been devastated. Tornados have a way of turning an outstanding day into your worst nightmare. While in Mexico, I was reminded of the brevity of life. Life is short, so we must be about our Father's business of witnessing to the lost and sharing the good news of salvation.

The Youngs, the missionaries who were escorting me around Mexico, asked if I wanted to stop and get a soda. They were kind enough to offer to buy me a Coke, but I informed them that I didn't drink soda, and I thanked them for their generosity. We found a spot to take our picture. I was wearing a tie-dyed T-shirt, of all things. We found a statue and took our picture.

When heading out of Mexico, we were bombarded by many people selling goods of many kinds. Many of the Mexican folks, both adults and children, were walking up and down beside the five to seven rows of cars trying to sell items. They would walk up to the window and start talking and sometimes tap the window to see if you were interested. The Youngs told me not to say anything, but to just keep looking forward. That's exactly what I did.

We finally got up to the border patrol station. The Youngs handed their passports to the female officer. For the record, I was grateful that the officer was a woman, because I thought she'd be more lenient on me since I had forgotten my passport. Boy, was I wrong! She gave me the hardest time about it—perhaps because she had to spend a few extra seconds looking up my information in her computer system. After she scolded me, I told her, "I'm sorry, officer. It won't happen again." I smiled and waved as we drove back into the United States of America.

We got back to the church in the late afternoon, and our team spent the rest of the evening relaxing. It was so good to take time to rest. Now whenever I hear Mexico mentioned, see it on a map, or hear people talk about it, I think back to my brief time spent there while cycling across America. I always laugh whenever I think about what happened at the border.

STORIES THAT MAKE ME SHAKE MY HEAD

I never anticipated that we would face so many thunderstorms. Greg and I were riding in Leakey, Texas. It was a good day in the saddle. We were both feeling good and enjoying the rolling hills of Texas. During our ride, we saw some clouds off in the distance. We figured the storm would intersect our path, but we remained positive, hoping it wouldn't hit us. The farther we rode, the darker the clouds got, and we realized that we would experience the rain. Rain in and of itself isn't bad, but the thunder and lightning got to us. I know there's rubber on bicycle tires, but it's much different riding through a storm on a bicycle than in a car. You feel protected in a car, or at least I do, but that's not the case on a bike.

As we started up a little climb with about ten miles to go to reach our destination, we heard a crack of thunder. I looked over at Greg and said something like "Well, I'm out, man. I'll see you soon." I laid down the power up that climb and used the momentum to zoom through the rolling hills. We were just in front of the storm, and it seemed like we were going to make it—when suddenly the roads opened up to another gorgeous mountaintop view. It was absolutely majestic! It was one of the most beautiful overlooks I've ever seen. The clouds were just starting to cover the area, the sky was darkening, and the trees were slowly being covered with shade. Immediately ahead was about a mile of descent with some switchbacks in the road. I looked back just before going down the hill, and I didn't see Greg or the motor home. At the bottom of the hill, the road took us through a field. There were a couple of houses there, and it was beginning to sprinkle. I could still hear the thunder, and it was getting closer.

As soon as I got to the small town of Leakey, the clouds started dumping rain. It was a complete downpour! The first shelter I found was at a motorcycle shop. I pulled into the parking lot and got under an awning. About five minutes later, I saw Greg in the distance. I began yelling, "Greg! Over here!" I was profusely waving my hands, hoping that he would see and hear me. He did. He rode through the parking lot, got off his bike, and took shelter with me under the awning. We had been close to outrunning the storm, but it caught us. We waited until the rain died down before loading up our bikes and driving to the cabin where we were staying that evening. I just shake my head every time I think about this adventurous episode from our trip.

Austin, Texas, makes me shake my head whenever I ponder the events that transpired there. Mindy was talking about how good the tacos were from a local Mexican restaurant chain. She insisted we were going to eat there. I analyzed the route and the locations of the fast-food restaurants, but there wasn't one close enough for us to detour on the bikes. I informed her that if she wanted to go, she'd have to use the rental car. She said that was fine, and she asked what we wanted. I remember saying, "Just get me five tacos."

Mindy, Elisabeth, and David went driving around town to get us some tacos. We had just ridden a good distance on the bicycles and were all starving. After catching up to Howard and Kevin in the RV at a gas station, we waited around an hour for them to meet back up with us. As you could imagine, each of the cyclists were ready to annihilate those tacos. Mindy, Elisabeth, and David finally entered the RV and passed out the tacos. We prayed over the food, and I remember asking, "Where's my other taco?"

They responded instantly, saying, "We only got you four." I was devastated, frustrated, and agitated all at the same time. All I could think about while I was eating those tacos was, *I wanted five, not four.* Just a word of advice: don't get in the way of a hungry cyclist. Honestly, I don't even remember the taste of the tacos because I was so disappointed that I didn't get five. Another inside joke developed from that incident: "Where's my taco?" Sometimes we'd start saying, "Hey, Greg. Where's my sandwich? Hey, Bryan. Where's my taco?" We laughed much about this on the trip.

God protected us while riding on highway 70 in Austin. Throughout the trip, we were constantly looking for shorter routes to travel. It sounds lazy, but it's not at all. Just try riding across America and see if you don't look for some shortcuts along the way. We would analyze the maps in detail and compare them to the GPS on our phones. If we noticed an alternate road to our next destination, we would give it serious consideration. It worked to our advantage one day on our way to Las Cruces, New Mexico, but it did not always work well.

We were on our way to Austin, Texas, and noticed highway 70 was a straight shot from the city to our next destination. It was a solid idea, in theory, but it turned out to be a bad idea in reality. It was my idea. Truthfully, the bad ideas on the trip were generally mine. I owned up to them—eventually. We got to Austin, Texas, and the traffic started to get heavy through downtown. I had expected as much, since it was one of the largest cities we would be traveling through.

All of a sudden, the highway opened up and turned into an interstate. Greg and I decided to keep going. The traffic was zooming by us at 70–80 mph. Ramps and exit ramps were popping up frequently. We were going 35–40 mph on the bicycles. I prayed at that moment, *God, please keep us safe.* After a couple of miles, we made the safe and wise decision to get off that road. We were able to safely exit the interstate without even a scratch. We stopped at a gas station to regroup and to figure out the route to the campground. God kept us safe and sovereignly protected us, even amid my foolish decisions.

One morning while in Texas, I got an early solo start since we had several pending obligations that day. The others slept in some and took time to rest. I ended up riding about forty miles by myself that day in the eastern part of Texas and almost into Louisiana. I remember seeing a cyclist ahead in the distance. At first, I thought it might be the female cyclist the guy in Arizona had told us about, but when I got closer, I could tell that there were two cyclists. I rode up beside them and startled them to death. I apologized and introduced myself. I told them what I was doing and gave them a tract. They informed me that they were a mother and daughter team. The young lady was a Girl Scout riding to benefit her troop. They had ridden over a thousand miles at the time I met them. After a brief conversation, I said goodbye, wished them well, and was off to pedal more miles.

I rode a few more miles, but I was out of water. I knew that I needed some liquids in my system, and I couldn't wait for the motor home. I saw a convenience store ahead on the left. I pulled off the road, walked up the steps, and set my bicycle on the porch before going inside. As soon as I walked in, a guy asked me, "Where you from?"

I said, "I'm from Roanoke, Virginia."

He instantly responded, "Me too." This didn't surprise me, because one of the pastors in Florida had family members in Roanoke. After some discussion, he finally admitted he was just kidding. Way to make me excited and then blow all the excitement away. Anyway, he then told me that he had done the same thing to a guy from England and that he had responded in a similar fashion. I shared with the folks in the store what I was doing and gave them each a tract.

In a few short minutes, that gentlemen (whose name I cannot remember) talked my ear off. He began to share how the folks in Louisiana talked too much and how they were a little "off." I remember thinking, *You're not too far behind them.* After a little more chatter, we parted ways, and all I could do was shake my head over that conversation.

CHAPTER 10

Louisiana: There Is Power in Prayer

There is no doubt that without the prayers of God's people, we would not have completed this rigorous adventure. Prayer played a major role throughout our trip across America. From beginning each ride with a time of prayer to our church family back home calling out our names to God, we experienced the power of prayer. God is a God who answers prayer. Christians can use prayer as a divine tool in the midst of spiritual warfare. Every believer is summoned by God to make earnest supplications to Him daily.

GOD ANSWERS PRAYER

Hindsight is 20/20. If I would have talked to some of the team members about my problem, they would have eased my worries and concerns. There it was again—more muscle spasms in my lungs. Elisabeth noticed the discomfort in my face during breakfast and asked about it. I was reluctant to talk to her about it, but she assured me it was muscle spasms. Sometimes endurance athletes get muscle cramps and spasms in the lungs, chest, and back. That's all it was, but I certainly wasn't expecting anything like it. In this moment, God answered a prayer of mine from earlier on the trip in DeRidder, Louisiana. I prayed, *God, please keep me healthy.* By His grace, I remained healthy the entire trip!

We had just finished our longest day of the trip. We had ridden 151 miles. That morning I woke up super early to make up about fifty miles we had lost due to inclement weather. Just imagine riding fifty miles on a bicycle and having another hundred to go. What was I thinking? Well, our adventure didn't have room for setbacks, so we pressed on in the power of God. Throughout that ride, my rear end was very uncomfortable. Due to the severe saddle sore I was experiencing, I would say that this was the third hardest day of the trip for me.

I am thankful that this was a flat route in Louisiana. If it had been full of elevation gain, it might have killed us. Dave and I closed off the last leg together. I clearly remember rolling into the parking lot of the Baptist church in DeRidder. The motor home was already parked and hooked up, but we couldn't find anybody. None of the support team members or other riders were in or around the RV.

I heard a door close and looked behind me. One of the church members had come out of the gymnasium and fellowship hall. After I told them who we were, they directed us into the gym to get some food. Their kitchen was full of volunteers who had prepared a wonderful meal. They fixed jambalaya, and it was divine! I had a hard time remembering what it was called, so I just called it "that Jumanji stuff."

After eating the wonderful food, I went to the pastor's house to shower. I'll try to be as discreet as possible, but when I looked at my backside in the mirror, there was a red rash about the size of Texas on my behind, and it really hurt. One of my cycling friends from Roanoke recommended applying a special ointment on saddle sores after each ride. Unfortunately, I didn't do that every day. I should have. That was a lesson learned in the ol' school of hard knocks.

That evening I applied half the bottle of special ointment to my backside. The next morning the rash was just about gone. I couldn't believe it. I had a praise and worship fest in the bathroom that morning. Each of the riders experienced saddle sores, and some days it caused them to have to abandon the entire day of riding. Even though we anticipated saddle sores and made preparations for them, there was nothing we could do but apply the ointments, persevere, and pray for God's healing.

The next morning, the church members cooked a classic American breakfast and even gave us lunch afterward. One of the ladies at the church told us that they made cheesecake at her bakery. I was really craving some cheesecake at the time, and she kindly brought us one. I was blown away by her generosity, but unfortunately, I never got to enjoy the cheesecake. The other team members devoured it before I could grab a bite. I heard it was delicious, though. Oh well. Maybe the next time I'm in DeRidder, I'll be able to try it. In addition to all the other hospitality and generosity from the people of this church, the congregation made a sizable contribution for our church's building fund. Their kindness blew me away. They taught me what it means to be hospitable!

On Sunday, June 21, we left DeRidder a little after 2:00 p.m. to adventure to Bunkie, Louisiana. It was not expected to be a long day. I predicted that we would make great time since it was flat, but we were not that fortunate. Aaron, Dave, Greg, and I rode together, and occasionally we were split into two groups. We experienced five flat tires and some mechanical problems that day. Dave and Aaron ended up riding in the car the last few miles due to frustrations with mechanical issues. Greg and I finished out the day.

The Baptist church in Bunkie was our destination, but due to the mechanical issues, we were way behind schedule. We contacted the church to inform them of our difficulties. We were riding through a rough section of Louisiana. People were using vulgar language toward us as we were cycling. Some would even give us cold stares. I'm just glad I wasn't alone that day. I remember praying silently, *Lord, please keep us safe.* The sun was setting during all of this, and it brought much tranquility to my mind. It reminded me that it doesn't matter how dark the world gets, the light of the gospel of Christ shines brightly!

After cycling through the rough section, Greg and I got separated from Aaron and Dave. The sun had finally set, and we were cruising in the dark. My light worked well, but we left it on the lowest setting because we didn't really know how many more miles we had to go. It was really hard reading the maps in the dark while riding. We were rotating pulls in a paceline, and somehow we completely missed our turn.[7] We went all the way to a stop sign that wasn't on our maps. There was a gas station across the road, but it was after 9:00 p.m. and the gas station was already closed. We stopped for a quick break to analyze the maps and the GPS on our phones.

It was completely dark outside. We were in the middle of nowhere in Louisiana at a closed gas station with stray cats meowing at us, and we were lost. We finally figured out which way to go. Mindy, Elisabeth, Aaron, and Dave were in the rental car. We were a few miles ahead of them. Since we had missed our turn and stopped, it didn't take long for them to catch us. When they did, we got them to drive behind us so we could use the lights of the car to see. It worked perfectly. There was minimal traffic, and we were almost to our destination.

At 10:00 p.m., we pulled into the parking lot of the Baptist church in Bunkie. I felt bad because we were extremely off schedule, but it was out of our control. Mechanical issues and flat tires had gotten the best of us that day. We did the best we could and worked through the problems. The church members had ordered pizza for us from Pizza Hut. Pizza never tasted so good! They also allowed us to stay in their spare house beside the church. The Christians in Louisiana demonstrated hospitality like I had never seen before. I had heard that the people down south were friendly, but this was far beyond my expectation. My life was forever impacted by their warm reception. Because of them, I now hope to demonstrate the same kindness to others.

After a wonderful night of rest, we woke up fully refreshed and ready to take on the day. I went inside to speak with the secretary. She was a very kind lady. I had spoken with her several times before while planning our stay. She gave me a tour of the facilities, and the stained-glass windows in their sanctuary were exquisite. They were blue and made the auditorium come to life. I took a few pictures to capture the memory. After the tour, the pastor requested that we stick around a little longer so we could meet some of the people. We had a brief, but

---

[7] A paceline is a formation in which riders (especially bicycle racers) travel in a line, one close behind the other, in order to conserve energy and travel faster by riding in the draft of the riders in front.

great, time of fellowship.

From allowing us to spend a night on their property to preparing gourmet meals, all the churches were a blessing to us. They truly demonstrated God's loving-kindness, grace, and mercy toward us while we were at their churches. They were even willing to let us minister God's Word to them. Please keep in mind that I had no prior connection with these churches. I had just cold-called them. Everything each congregation did for us helped me to better understand the role of pastoring and how Christians are called to hospitality. I'm grateful to God that these assemblies were willing to embrace my unexpected phone calls.

Anyone who says that God doesn't answer prayer has not spent much time with Him in prayer. Our trip across the United States of America is an affirmed testimony of God's direct answer to prayer. Our team could not have accomplished all we did without God's divine intervention. We, as a team and as a church, humbly asked God to protect, guide, use, and help us as we sought to tell others about His gospel and raise finances for a new building.

I set out to accomplish many goals while on this trip in addition to my goal of cycling one hundred miles per day. I was overzealous in several areas. One of those areas in which I was not overzealous was in keeping a prayer journal. I certainly spent time in prayer, and our team spent time in prayer together, but with all that was going on, I was unable to spend as much quality time journaling my prayers as I would have liked to. Prayer journaling is a practice I started while in college and continue to this day. I'd recommend that you do the same. It really helps me focus when meditating on the Scriptures and in prayer with the Savior. I did manage to journal some days, though.

Here is my prayer-journal entry from May 27, 2015, written at about 9:30 p.m.:

> Lord, thank you so very much for the amazing opportunity to travel from coast to coast on a bicycle to capture the world's attention to declare the message of salvation.

Please give us the strength that we need, safety, and open doors to share the gospel. I am so excited I can't even contain myself right now. As you very well know, Lord, I have put a lot of time, energy, and effort into this trip, and my prayer is that all of the hard work will bring glory, honor, and praise to the Lord Jesus Christ. Please help us get through these next few days because I know they are going to be challenging. A few people have shared Psalm 91:11 with me, which says, "For he shall give his angels charge over thee, to keep thee in all thy ways." God, may Your protective hand always be upon us during the next several days as we travel. Thank You, Lord, for laying it upon a couple people's hearts to share this verse of Scripture with me. Please give me a good night's sleep, and help me to honor You in everything that I say and do.

God answered this prayer on many days of our trip. His sovereign hand of protection was upon us every moment of every day. He was there to protect us when we traveled through unfamiliar areas. God protected us during inclement weather. He shielded us from the enemy's attacks to divide us. He guarded us under the shadow of His sovereign wings. God answered our prayers of protection. Jesus Christ can do the same for you.

I'm reminded of Acts 1:14: "These all continued with one accord in prayer and supplication, *with the women*, and Mary the mother of Jesus, and with his brethren" (emphasis added). Women have vital roles to play in ministry, and one of those roles is prayer. Some of the greatest prayer warriors I've met are women. God showed me through this experience that He answers prayer from all His children, including women.

We were traveling in Louisiana, getting ready to cross the Mississippi River. Crossing the bridge over the river was the highest elevation point on the day's ride. Our place to stay in Jackson, Louisiana, fell through, and we had to search for a new place. This wasn't an easy task. Howard and Kevin began to search for RV parks, but all were full or not worth staying in. The sun was about to set, and we still had no clue where we were going to sleep. I knew we would figure things out because God hadn't let us down yet, but some of our team members were pretty distraught. I remember stopping just before the Mississippi River bridge to fill our water bottles and eat a snack. That was when Mindy suggested we have a time of prayer. She led us to the throne of God. It was a powerful moment, and as soon as she said, "Amen," we knew God was going to intervene.

Man, woman, boy, or girl can go to God in prayer always expecting God to answer. Please know that God answers our prayers according to His will (1 John 5:14–15), and sometimes His will does not coincide with our requests. Never neglect the sweet hour of prayer.

PRAYER IS OUR SPIRITUAL WEAPON

Imagine a soldier going into combat without his weapon. In today's age of warfare, some sort of firepower is mandatory. Have you heard of the saying "Don't bring a knife to a gunfight"? In our modern world, war demands heavy firepower. A soldier going into battle without a gun would be suicide. In like manner, a Christian going into spiritual warfare without prayer is like committing spiritual suicide. Prayer is the secret weapon for the child of God. Ephesians 6:18 says, "*Praying always* with all prayer and supplication in the Spirit, and watching thereunto with all perseverance and supplication for all saints" (emphasis added). Wearing the entire armor of God without the power of prayer is complete foolishness.

As a minister, I understood the significant role that prayer would play throughout this cycling mission trip. After meditating in God's Word and prayer, I was compelled to request daily prayer for our team from the members of Clearbrook Baptist Church. While some believers were sent to witness, others were left behind to pray. I had devised a prayer schedule for the church members back home so they could faithfully pray for us. The gravity of prayer cannot be discounted. It ranged from 4:00 a.m. to 11:30 p.m. I asked forty people to commit to stopping whatever they were doing to pray for us at the same time every day during the month of June. I believe the many prayers of God's people provided renewed strength for our team members. Here is what the schedule looked like:

Prayer Team for Bike Missions Trip
Sunday–Saturday for June 1–30

4:00 a.m.: _____   4:30 a.m.: _____

5:00 a.m.: _____   5:30 a.m.: _____

6:00 a.m.: _____   6:30 a.m.: _____

7:00 a.m.: _____   7:30 a.m.: _____

8:00 a.m.: _____   8:30 a.m.: _____

9:00 a.m.: _____   9:30 a.m.: _____

10:00 a.m.: _____   10:30 a.m.: _____

11:00 a.m.: _____   11:30 a.m.: _____

12:00 p.m.: _____   12:30 p.m.: _____

1:00 p.m.: _____   1:30 p.m.: _____

2:00 p.m.: _____   2:30 p.m.: _____

3:00 p.m.: _____   3:30 p.m.: _____

4:00 p.m.: _____   4:30 p.m.: _____

5:00 p.m.: _____   5:30 p.m.: _____

6:00 p.m.: _____   6:30 p.m.: _____

7:00 p.m.: _____   7:30 p.m.: _____

8:00 p.m.: _____   8:30 p.m.: _____

9:00 p.m.: _____   9:30 p.m.: _____

10:00 p.m.: _____   10:30 p.m.: _____

11:00 p.m.: _____   11:30 p.m.: _____

I did not ask the members of the prayer team to pray for any designated length of time. I'm sure some of the prayer warriors spent much more than the allotted time in prayer, but I am also certain that some days, the amount of time was much shorter. It did not matter how long someone spent in prayer; what mattered was that someone prayed for us. Looking at the schedule, you're probably thinking, *Who in the world would be up at 4:00 a.m.?* Well, to my surprise, the early morning hours were the first to be filled. By the way, I asked the members not to put names on the sign-up sheet, but to just put a check mark beside the time. I did this for two reasons: First, I wanted multiple people to sign up for the same time allotment because you can never have too many people praying. Second, I did not want to give an opportunity for vainglory by having someone writing their name in for a specific time. I wanted everything to be anonymous. When or how long someone spends in prayer is a private matter.

When contemplating all of this, my mind was drawn to the words of Christ in Matthew 6:5–6:

> And when thou prayest, thou shalt not be as the hypocrites are: for they love to pray standing in the synagogues and in the corners of the streets, that they may be seen of men. Verily I say unto you, They have their reward. But thou, when thou prayest, enter into thy closet, and when thou hast shut thy door, pray to thy Father which is in secret; and thy Father which seeth in secret shall reward thee openly.

Fasting is another secret weapon Christians can use in spiritual warfare. Whether you want to admit it or not, we are in a spiritual battle every single day. Sometimes we succeed, and sometimes we fail. Ephesians 6:12 says, "For we wrestle not against flesh and blood, but against principalities, against powers, against the rulers of the darkness of this world, *against spiritual wickedness in high places*" (emphasis added). Prayer and fasting is a practice that modern Christians often neglect, but it is something God has called us to do.

The disciples were commissioned to do a variety of things. In Matthew 17 they were attempting to cast out demonic spirits. They attempted to do so but failed. They were frustrated because of this. After they observed Christ casting the spirit out of the man who was possessed, the disciples asked Christ, "Why could not we cast him out?" (Matthew 17:19). Jesus responded, *"Because of your unbelief: for verily I say unto you, If ye have faith as a grain of mustard seed, ye shall say unto this mountain, Remove hence to yonder place; and it shall remove; and nothing shall be impossible unto you. Howbeit this kind goeth not out but by prayer and fasting"* (Matthew 17:20–21, emphasis added).

The Lord Jesus Christ revealed that when faith is combined with prayer and fasting, you can move mountains. In other words, it is possible to accomplish great and mighty things in Jesus's name. After pondering this, I decided to not only have a prayer team, but to also have a fasting team. There are three meals in each day: breakfast, lunch, and dinner. I requested that twenty-one people sign up to fast for one meal per week for the month of June. This time of fasting would be dedicated to extra prayer on behalf of our team. For example, if someone signed up for breakfast on Sunday, they were committing to fast every Sunday during breakfast during the month of June. Instead of eating the meal, the church member would spend the time asking for God's protection, guidance, renewed strength, assistance, and other special requests on behalf of our team.

I used the same anonymity method by asking the church members to put check marks next to the list meals for the day. Matthew 6:16–18 says:

> Moreover *when ye fast,* be not, as the hypocrites, of a sad countenance: for they disfigure their faces, that they may appear unto men to fast. Verily I say unto you, They have their reward. But thou, when thou fastest, anoint thine head, and wash thy face; that thou appear not unto men to fast, but unto thy Father which is in secret: and thy

Father, which seeth in secret, shall reward thee openly.
(Emphasis added)

I was amazed at the response from our church family, who signed up to fast and pray for us as we pedaled from coast to coast. Here is what the sign-up sheet looked like:

Fasting Team for Bike Missions Trip
Sunday–Saturday for June 1–30

Sunday Breakfast: _____

Sunday Lunch: _____

Sunday Dinner: _____

Monday Breakfast: _____

Monday Lunch: _____

Monday Dinner: _____

Tuesday Breakfast: _____

Tuesday Lunch: _____

Tuesday Dinner: _____

Wednesday Breakfast: _____

Wednesday Lunch: _____

Wednesday Dinner: _____

Thursday Breakfast: _____

Thursday Lunch: _____

Thursday Dinner: _____

Friday Breakfast: _____

Friday Lunch: _____

Friday Dinner: _____

Saturday Breakfast: _____

Saturday Lunch: _____

Saturday Dinner: _____

Another way our church family prayed for us was by laying hands on our team members the last Sunday we were at church before the trip.

I asked for all the team members to come to the front of the church auditorium for a special time of prayer during the evening service on Sunday, May 24, 2015. I requested all the men in the church to come and lay their hands upon our cycling mission team and pray for us. Two of the men in our assembly lifted up their voices to God on our behalf. We witnessed the power of prayer on this trip.

MAKE PRAYER A DAILY PRACTICE

After eating the pizza in Bunkie, Louisiana, we got settled into the parsonage where we were staying for the night. Most of us had our own room. It was a good feeling to be sleeping in a room all by myself. I remember waking up during the night and realizing that my air mattress was completely deflated. I had no clue what had gone wrong. Perhaps I didn't seal the cap tight enough, or maybe I had not put enough air in it. Nonetheless, the air pump was right next to me. I had used the air pump earlier, and it did not seem very loud. I grabbed the cable, plugged the cord into the wall, put the hose in the air mattress, and turned it on. The noise sounded like a chainsaw. I prayed, *God, please don't let this wake anybody up.*

A few moments later, I heard Greg moaning in the other room. I thought, *Oh, great. I woke up Greg and made him mad. I'll apologize to everyone in the morning.* I finished using the pump, set the machine to the side, and went back to sleep.

After everyone was up, ready, and about to eat breakfast, I told them I needed to talk to them about something. I went through the whole story of how I had awakened during the night to find my mattress deflated and had to pump it back up. I said, "I'm really sorry for the loud racket last night. I didn't realize the air pump was as loud as it was. When we get to St. Augustine, I'm going to buy everybody ice cream for the disturbance." They looked at me and said, "Thank you, Bryan, but we didn't hear anything last night." We had a good laugh, but they held me to my word the last evening of the trip. I bought every team member some ice cream.

When I was contacting churches, I talked with a pastor from Jackson, Louisiana, who said he didn't see why our team couldn't stay on their property, but he'd have to get it approved in their business meeting. Since I'm also the pastor of a Baptist church with monthly business meetings, I completely understood. I contacted him a few weeks later regarding their decision, but he said he had forgotten to bring it up. He affirmed that he'd do so in the next meeting. I tried to reach him numerous times during the following weeks, but to no avail.

The day finally arrived when we were leaving Bunkie, Louisiana, to travel to Jackson, and I was finally able to reach the pastor on the phone. He shared with me that Hollywood was filming a movie in the area, and their church wouldn't allow the filming crew to stay on church property during the production. He said that since they were not letting the filming crew stay on their property, they couldn't allow us to stay either. Completely understanding his plight, I bid him adieu and told him to have a great day. After informing my team of this, most of our attitudes were not in the best of shape. I reassured them that everything would be okay. This was the only day of the trip when we were clueless as to where we were going to stay the night. Our prayers were answered when we finally found a motel to stay in outside of Jackson.

Our mental attitude determines our spiritual altitude. Isaiah 26:3 says, "Thou wilt keep him in perfect peace, whose mind is stayed on thee: because he trusteth in thee." Just like we discovered on our cross-country bicycle ride, we all will face moments when our attitudes will be challenged. Sometimes we'll do things out of habit rather than with gratefulness. There will be moments when we go through the motions of reading the Bible, spending time in prayer, or attending worship services instead of doing it from a heart of worship to God. Developing a Christlike attitude begins by thinking like Him. In order to have an attitude like Christ, we have to ask ourselves these questions:

What would Jesus do in this situation?

How would Christ respond?

What would Christ's attitude be?

Allow obstacles to help you develop an attitude like Christ's. Is your attitude hindering or helping your relationship with Christ? Attitude determines altitude.

Just as brushing your teeth, taking a shower, using deodorant, styling your hair, and getting dressed are daily routines, so God calls believers to make prayer a daily practice. Before we would set out on our rides, we devoted time to prayer. Some days we only prayed once prior to adventuring out on the roads, and sometimes we prayed many times throughout the day as a team. This was important, not just to me, but to our entire team. We regularly prayed for God's protection, direction, and provision. We depended fully on God for these matters. Yes, we made the proper preparations for the trip, but if God isn't in our plans, then it's best not to use those plans.

One day Greg and I went into a gas station while Aaron went to get a snack and Mindy filled up the rental car with gas. I remember eating chicken nuggets and drinking a smoothie. It was a great snack. While Greg and I were in the gas station hunting down the beverages, a guy came up to us complimenting our cycling jerseys. It wasn't the first time somebody did that, but this was different. This man, Forrest, began to share a little about himself. He told us that he was a Christian and that he felt led to talk to us and encourage us. We told him that we were cycling across America, and we explained our purpose.

He thought it was awesome. In the middle of the gas station, Forrest asked us if he could pray for us. We had a prayer meeting in the gas station. It was a God moment, for sure. I sensed the presence of God's Spirit upon us during that prayer. We gave Forrest a tract as a reminder to pray for us, and we parted ways. I was pretty pumped about it and immediately told Aaron and Mindy what had just happened. When we got to our destination that evening, I told the rest of the team about it as well. It was really encouraging to know there are still people all across the United States who are not ashamed to pray in public in the name of Jesus.

Often on the trip, I used my bicycle riding time as a time of prayer. While climbing some of the highest mountains, I would continually ask God for strength to make it to the top. During our battles with headwinds, I frequently had complaining sessions with God. I'd often pray, *Please make the winds stop, God.* Sometimes they'd cease, and sometimes they continued howling on. While cycling alone, I'd use the time as an opportunity to simply talk to God.

There were a few days when I rode every mile alone, and the prayer sessions with Christ got me through. On the 120-plus mile days, I often resorted to prayer. I'm sure God was glad when the ride was over because He wouldn't have to hear my voice for a few hours. For the record, God doesn't view our prayer time with Him in that manner.

Through this experience, God revealed to me that we can talk to Him no matter our situation or circumstance. Of course, I already knew this biblical truth, but God reminded me in a way I had never noticed before. Sometimes we get the idea that we can only pray during a church service or in front of the altar. That's just not the reality. Believers can go to God at any time and in any place. Whether you're lying in bed, driving down the road, sitting in a park, riding your bicycle, or walking on a greenway, you can pray to God. Hebrews 4:16 says, "Let us therefore come boldly unto the throne of grace, that we may obtain mercy, and find grace to help in time of need."

May I be so bold to ask, How is your prayer life? If you're like most believers, it's an area that could use some improvement. Spend time every day talking to God in prayer. Talk to Him about everything. Figure out what works best for you, and do it regularly. If you need a prayer partner, find one. If you need a prayer journal, keep one. If you need to wake up early or stay up late, do it. You will never regret the moments you spend with the Lord in prayer. God is a God who answers prayer. Prayer is our weapon in the spiritual battle. Make prayer a daily habit and practice of your Christian walk. Pray about everything. Philippians 4:6 says, "Be careful for nothing; but *in everything* by prayer and supplication with thanksgiving *let your requests be made known unto God*" (emphasis added).

CHAPTER 11
Mississippi and Alabama: You Live and Learn

In the middle of Mississippi, I had another flat tire. Aaron, Greg, and Dave were all riding with me that day. Sometimes we'd all stop when someone got a flat. Other times we would just slow the pace down to give the person time to change the tire and catch up. I remember telling the guys, "I've got a flat. Just keep going, and I'll catch up." Sometimes changing flats went smoothly, and sometimes it was quite an obstacle. For some reason, this time I was having trouble getting the tire back onto the rim. I was sitting on the side of the road, my bike was upside down, and my hands were solid black from the grease. I guess I looked like a bike mechanic that day. One person even stopped and asked if I was okay. I assured them I was fine and that it was only a flat tire, and I thanked them for their kindness. It probably only took about thirty minutes, but it seemed like an eternity.

After finally finishing the task, I began pedaling at a faster pace than normal to catch up with the guys. It was fun for me to pick up the pace occasionally because I would sometimes get bored riding at a casual pace. I rode a few miles and saw a cyclist on the side of the road changing his tire. From a distance, it looked like he was wearing a white jersey like mine. Sure enough, it was Greg. I'm glad I was there, because he was in need of my small pump. By the way, this pump was the worst pump you could use to fill the tires with air. You could pump it thirty times and barely have fifty psi in the tube, and we generally put around one hundred psi in them. It was frustrating to use, but it managed to get us to the support team for a real pump.

I believe each of these mechanical issues helped strengthen our relationships because we had to learn to trust each other. In the same way, our relationship with Christ can increase and improve as we learn to trust Him more. It all begins with trusting Christ for salvation and what He's done on the cross for us because of our sins. Acts 16:31 says, "Believe on the Lord Jesus Christ, and thou shalt be saved." The term *believe* literally means "to entrust." Nobody will be able to spend eternity in heaven without trusting Christ as Lord and Savior.

"Live and learn" has been a phrase that has stuck with me ever since I first heard it. Life is about living and learning. Sometimes we live to learn, and other times we learn to live. Some people learn in the school of hard knocks, while others learn by observation. Both schools are great to gain knowledge from, but it's best to learn from observation. People are oftentimes hardheaded and unwilling to learn by listening. There were many things God showed me on this cycling expedition, and I want to share three of them with you now.

The Bible Is Our Roadmap

During my research for the trip, I came across the Adventure Cycling Association. This group exists for many reasons, but what grabbed my attention was their cycling maps across the United States. As I mentioned earlier, they had documented three main routes: the Northern Tier Route, the TransAmerica Trail, and the Southern Tier Route. You can also use the Western Express (San Francisco, CA, to Pueblo, CO) and connect with the TransAmerica Trail from Colorado to Virginia. So technically, there are four coast-to-coast routes. The Northern Tier Route is 4,239 miles, the TransAmerica Trail is 4,228 miles, the Western Express combined with the TransAmerica is about 3,500 miles, and the Southern Tier Route is 3,055 miles. After analyzing the mileage and confirming our allotted days of travel, we decided on traveling the Southern Tier since we wanted to make the trip in thirty days.

When I received the maps in the mail, I was super stoked. I tore open the box, unfolded each of the maps, and started calculating all the logistics. During that process, I noticed that the maps were copyrighted in 2011. It was 2015 when I bought them. Without thinking too much about it, I thought, *Well, I'm sure not much has changed in a few years with these routes.* In addition to the main maps, I was sent several extra papers where changes had been made.

I mentioned Phil Keoghan's cycling trip earlier. When he began, he left Los Angeles with great energy and excitement—until he was asked at a stoplight, "Hey, Phil. Which way do I turn?" He had been so consumed with training, planning the logistics, and scheduling events that he had forgotten to study the maps or appoint someone to analyze them in detail. That part of Phil's documentary was humorous, but I knew I didn't want to make the same mistake.

I learned from Phil's mistake and studied the maps thoroughly. I did not have them memorized, but I perused them several times. I presented our team with three options to choose from. This demonstrated to the team that I had studied the maps, and I provided input to help the team decide which route we were going to take. Even though I had studied the Southern Tier maps thoroughly, I had failed to analyze the extra papers that had additional directions. Perhaps that would have helped when we got turned around a few times. Oh well. You live and learn.

In every major city we rode through, we got lost. It wasn't just the cyclists who got turned around. Howard and Kevin got lost in the motor home too. Honestly, I was surprised we didn't get lost in San Diego, but the maps were very clear in that section. The first city we got lost in was Phoenix. Greg and I were trying to find a greenway, but we kept missing the turn for it. I'm sure the maps being four years outdated had something to do with it. We kept riding up and down the same road for almost an hour. Oddly enough, we could see the greenway off in the distance in what seemed to be a large drainage dip, but we could not locate the entrance. I was also confused when I saw three bicycle paths in the same location. There were two on each end of the drainage dip and one going directly in the middle. The maps didn't show all of that, and it confused us to the max. We finally managed to find the greenway, and we pressed on. While we were disoriented trying to find the bike path, the support team was having great difficulty navigating through the big city of Phoenix. From what I understand, the brand-new GPS took them in circles around the same blocks.

When Greg and I were in El Paso, Texas, our maps did not match the road. We arrived at the exact location on the map, but the next intersection was completely different from what was indicated on the actual road. I got tired of reading an inaccurate map and comparing it with the GPS app on my phone, so I decided to ask someone for help. The first person I approached was an older Hispanic man. He seemed like a really nice guy, but he didn't speak any English. We talked to a few people, but none of them spoke English well enough to have a conversation with us. I remember raising my voice slightly while pointing at my map, but that didn't help at all. Isn't it funny how we think people who speak other languages can understand what we're saying if we speak louder? We decided to keep riding, and we finally found where the maps picked up.

Another time while riding, I heard my phone ding in my back pocket. I pulled the phone out and saw a text from Mindy and Elisabeth in the rental car with this question: "Are you sure we're going the right way?" Sometimes it can be hard to admit you are wrong, and this was one of those times. I don't know why, but it was. We had just taken a left turn. Aaron, Dave, Greg, and I were pedaling with force, but the left turn was a wrong turn. I had misread the maps and directed the crew in the wrong direction. After riding a couple of miles, we decided to pull over and look at the maps more carefully. Sure enough, I had made a wrong turn.

I'd like to add that it can be difficult to read a map while riding a bicycle. The wind was blowing every which way, which surely didn't help. Picture a guy riding down the road with no hands on the handlebars and an unfolded map in his hands. That was me some days, but most days I folded the map in a way that I could read it with one hand. I remember drifting back to the rental car and saying, "Thanks, ladies. You saved the day."

Life has a way of taking wrong turns, or at least they seem like wrong turns at the time. I'm a firm believer that everything happens for a reason. Romans 8:28 teaches us that God works out all things for good for believers in the gospel. GPS systems, maps, and other directional devices are surely wrong sometimes. I was led astray by them a few times on this trip, but God's Word is our roadmap for life. If you want to be directed by Jesus Christ every step of your life, then you need to allow Him to do so through His Word. The Bible is every believer's roadmap for their life. Psalm 37:23 says, "The steps of a good man are ordered by the LORD: and he delighteth in his way."

TAKE TIME TO REST

God protected me when I was stranded in a severe thunderstorm in Mississippi. We had some back-to-back days of 120 miles in Louisiana and Mississippi. The other guys wanted to ride both days but weren't able to ride all the miles. They rode a solid seventy miles and decided to call it a day since they were going to attempt to ride all the miles the next day. After a short break, I took off to finish the day. The support car was several miles down the road getting some groceries, and the RV suddenly passed right by me.

I was all by myself when I heard the thunder crackling in the distance. I could see it all in the distance but was hoping to make it over the little hill to the next town before stopping. I picked up the pace and laid down the hammer. I saw a large bolt of lightning in the sky, followed by thunder. I immediately decided it was time to find a place of refuge. I noticed a little driveway leading into a fence. Inside the fence, there were a couple of sheds. I figured I would hop the fence and take shelter until the storm passed.

As soon as I got off the bike, a few dogs that were inside the fence came charging at me. I don't play with dogs, especially when they aren't friendly and appear to be craving me for lunch. The dogs were growling, barking, showing me their teeth, and jumping on the fence. I made the executive decision to not go over the fence. A few moments later, in addition to the lightning and thunder, the rain began to pour down. Those crazy dogs stopped all their ruckus and darted straight for the shelter. I just shook my head, wishing I could join them.

I had to make a choice. Should I stay under the large tree or get underneath a bunch of bushes? I chose the bushes. Yes, I was aware that hiding under a tree or some bushes was not the safest place in a storm, but I wasn't willing to get devoured by a bunch of dogs either. As soon as I knelt in front of the bushes, the rain began to pour. It poured like I've never seen it pour before.

During all this, I was trying to call the others to tell them that I was stranded in a storm and needed a safe place for shelter, but no one was answering their phones. Go figure, right? The moment you need someone, not a soul answers the phone. Immediately after that, I sent texts to the support team. The thunder was booming, the lightning bolts were striking, and the rain was pounding down. I finally got in touch with Aaron. He and Mindy were coming to get me in the support car, but because of all the noise, I couldn't hear them on the phone. I tried to tell them where I was. I did the best I could under the circumstances.

I'll never forget the moment they drove past me. I jolted out from under the bush, screaming as loudly as I could, "Aaron! Mindy! I'm right here!" I was waving my arms in the air and jumping up and down while shining my bicycle light toward the oncoming traffic. I know what you're thinking. *Why didn't you just call them?* Well, that was the problem. My phone had gotten wet, and I was unable to use it. I couldn't text, call, or use it in any way. They called every minute, and I couldn't answer. I was literally stranded. I finally decided to just crawl back under the bush and wait for the storm to pass.

After I kneeled under the bushes, I saw a lightning bolt strike to my left, less than the length of a football field away. I rarely get scared, but I don't remember ever being more frightened in my life. *Will I get struck by lightning? Will a tree fall on me? Is anyone going to stop and check on me? Is the storm ever going to end? Am I going to die?* My anxiety got the best of me, and I began to quiver. Perhaps it was due to the cold rain, but my hunch is it was because I was afraid.

I felt like Martin Luther when he surrendered to become a monk. Luther was traveling down the road when a severe thunderstorm came his way. He was afraid for his life. If you've ever been stranded in a storm without protection or shelter, then you know what it's like. Luther fell to the ground and prayed to God in surrender to His will. I remember praying, *Lord, please protect me. Get me through this storm. If You get me through this storm, I'll serve You the rest of my life. In Jesus's name, Amen.* This was not a silent prayer, nor was it a whispering prayer. I was screaming it out loud at the top of my lungs.

The thunder finally started to sound farther away, and I could no longer see the lightning. It was still raining, but not like it had been. The cars were no longer going less than 30 mph but were back to their regular speed. To Aaron and Mindy's relief, I was finally able to answer my phone. I told them that by the time I had tried waving them down, they were already gone. They turned around and picked me up. I was very relieved to see them pull that rental car in the driveway where I was hiding out. As I shivered, they gave me some towels and told me to warm up in the car. It was Mississippi in the month of June, and I wanted the heat on in the vehicle.

While I was in the car replaying the scene in my mind, I could not believe that no one had stopped to see if I was okay. I had my one-hundred-dollar bicycle light on in flashing mode facing the oncoming traffic. It was sitting on my Giant in the driveway next to the road. Every time a car went by, I would say to myself, *Please stop. Please stop. Please stop.* Surprisingly, no one did. I guess it was raining so hard they couldn't see the light.

While I was in the car recuperating from having been stranded in a severe thunderstorm, one man pulled over and asked if everything was all right. He had noticed my flashing light as he was driving by, and he decided to turn around to check it out. That was very thoughtful. I think Aaron and Mindy eventually told him what we were doing and gave him one of our fliers.

Physically, I could have ridden another seventy miles that day, but mentally, I was done. It doesn't matter how strong you are or how great of shape you are in; as soon as you're conquered mentally, there is no chance for success. I experienced this after the storm. I didn't want to ride the bike anymore for the rest of the day. After all that I had just been through, I made the decision to relax for the rest of the day. I couldn't gain the mental stability to finish out the day. I needed to regroup mentally.

Aaron and Mindy drove me to the Magnolia Spring Assembly of God church in Hurley, Mississippi, where we were attending service that Wednesday evening. I told them that I would just make up the extra fifty miles the next day. Sometimes we are forced to rest even though we don't want to.

Looking back at that dramatic experience, I saw God's sovereign hand of protection each moment. I thought I had needed refuge under a shelter or in a vehicle, but now I know that God's providential hand was protecting me during the thunderstorm. I learned a valuable lesson: God protects His children during the storms of life. If God sheltered me during the storm I faced, then I know, with all surety, that God is able to protect you from every storm you encounter in life.

Jesus was a very busy man during His earthly ministry. He was out preaching to the lost. He was recruiting followers and teaching His heavenly oracles. Christ was busy casting out demonic spirits, healing the sick, raising the dead, giving sight to the blind, feeding the hungry, giving hearing to the deaf, giving strength to the lame, and praying for those in need. The ministry efforts of Christ were very taxing on His physical body. Mark 1:35 says, "And in the morning, rising up a great while before day, he went out, and departed into a solitary place, and there prayed." Jesus knew the importance of secluding Himself from society in a solitary place. Taking time to rest in solitude is one of the most overlooked areas of ministry.

Today's culture is enamored with being busy. People say, "The busier you are, the more successful you will be." This is not necessarily true. There are plenty of people who have no time for leisure who aren't successful. Some people are consumed with busy lifestyles in order to pay bills, and they're barely scraping by. Being busy is not bad; it's actually a good thing.

One preacher said, "An idle mind is the devil's workshop."[8] Those who remain idle may fall prey to the temptation of the devil; however, being busy is about quality, not quantity. Jesus Christ's earthly ministry was one of ministering to the masses, but He invested in twelve people. He spent the majority of His time with the twelve disciples, and the world was shaken by His efforts. We are still reaping from what Christ sowed into those twelve men's lives.

Mark 1:35 affirms the importance of taking time to rest. If Jesus Christ rested, then so should we. Modern Christianity, at least Westernized Christianity, has become captive to extreme busyness in ministry. Perhaps this is the reason why there are so many shallow Christians in the church today. More is accomplished by doing less. Investing in fewer people accomplishes much more than trying to invest in everybody. Jesus knew this, and that's why He practiced it. I knew all of this while planning our trip, but as much as I hate to admit it, we were too busy.

I'm reminded of Mark 6:31: "And he said unto them, Come ye yourselves apart into a desert place, and rest a while: for there were many coming and going, and they had no leisure so much as to eat." If Jesus Christ and the disciples took time to rest, then it's important for us to do the same. Far too many times in our Christian walk, we become consumed with busyness and we forget to rest. The disciples

---

[8.] It seems that the first use of this was by the Puritan William Perkins in 1603, when he wrote, "The idle body and the idle brain is the shop of the devil." In H. G. Bohn's 1855 *Handbook of Proverbs*, he wrote, "An idle brain is the devil's workshop."

did this, and Christ called them out.

Our journey was awesome, but one of our mistakes was that we were too busy. When I thought of this verse, I almost felt as if Christ was speaking directly to our team. Yes, we are called by God to share the gospel, make disciples, study His Word, etc., but God has also called us to take time to rest. In fact, we were so busy on the trip that we didn't have much time for our own spiritual walk with the Lord. Most days, all I had time for was the daily verse of Scripture on the YouVersion app. That's better than nothing, but it's not very much spiritual nourishment. Nonetheless, one great spiritual lesson that I learned was to take time to rest. Do yourself a favor and take quality time to rest.

TOGETHER EVERYONE ACHIEVES MORE

Our team's theme was "Biking the USA for Yahweh." We made a great team together, but the greatest teammate of our trip was Jesus Christ. Because we worked together as a team, we were able to accomplish much more than if we had not worked together. When we worked together as a team, I believe God brought His hand of blessing and protection upon us because He desires His people to dwell together in harmony. Psalm 133:1 says, "Behold, how good and how pleasant it is for brethren to dwell together in unity!"

God protected Dave when he got a nail in his tire. There we were, cycling through Mobile, Alabama. It was a beautiful city full of life, but when we crossed the bay, it stunk to high heaven. Whew! I've never smelled anything that could produce something that potent before in my life. I had anticipated cycling over a majestic bay, but when I looked into the water, I noticed how dirty it was. While crossing the bay, I got separated from the guys because I was trying to soak in the scenery. From the ginormous ships in the sea to the beautiful blue sky, you could say I was a little distracted from riding my bike.

Aaron, Greg, and Dave kept pulling away. I saw them about a half mile ahead of me, and they had deviated slightly from the map. I took the correct way and ended up in front of them. I told them that I needed a restroom break. After making sure that they had the directions to our dwelling place, I told them to go on, assuring them that I would catch up. I stopped at a nearby hotel. For the record, hotels have much nicer bathrooms than gas stations. I even carried my bicycle with me into the restroom. I'm sure the employees thought I was strange, but I wasn't going to chance anybody stealing my bicycle. It was my only transportation, for crying out loud.

After taking care of business, I picked up the pace slightly to catch up with the guys. I went a couple of miles and saw a cyclist on the side of the road. It's always a good practice to stop to make sure they are okay. As I got closer, I realized it was Dave. He had a flat tire. I helped him change his tire, and we were back on the road. Greg and Aaron, by that time, were quite a distance ahead of us. Even though we were separated, it was all right. We just kept going.

We caught up to the RV with Kevin, Howard, and David. We ate a snack, refilled our water bottles, and asked if they had seen Aaron and Greg. They had not. I contacted them to make sure they were on the right road and had enough water and snacks. They were in good shape. Dave and I kept moving forward, but Dave's tire kept losing air, so we had to stop every little bit to pump it up. Finally, we pulled into a gas station to change the tube. I went inside and bought some more smoothies. The best part about these drinks is that they offer three hundred to five hundred calories per bottle, and since they are liquid, you don't even have to take a bite. You just guzzle them down and refuel.

While I went into the store, Dave began the preparation work to replace the flat. I remember telling him, "This is our last tube. Let's pray we don't get another flat." At that moment, a guy pulled over to the side of the road to check on us. We told him our dilemma, and he gave us some black construction tape. Dave put it inside his tire in a couple of spots, and it did the trick. We took some time to share with the guy what we were doing and gave him one of our fliers. He went on his way, and we started riding again.

Keep in mind that Dave and I had both of the bicycle pumps but no spare tubes. We happened to be the two who had been issued the pumps, in case we got separated and encountered mechanical difficulties. Aaron and Greg had no pump, and thankfully, they didn't get any flats. As soon as we left the gas station, we rode the rest of the ride on perfectly smooth pavement. For the most part, we rode on horribly maintained roads. Perhaps that's why we were constantly getting flat tires.

During all this, the support team was confirming our campground lodging. We didn't plan on staying the night in Alabama, but it also didn't work out for us to stay in Pensacola, Florida, so we ended up staying in a campground next to the Florida state line. God offered protection for all of us in Alabama. God always protects His children, and we were no exception. Just as He protected us during our circumstances, He can do the same for you.

Teamwork makes the dream work. There is no "I" in team. For most of my life, I've tried to do things on my own. Most of the time it works out well, but I knew this trip couldn't be done solely by one person. We needed teamwork to make this mission trip work. I recognized this early on and sought to figure out ways to lighten each team member's workload on the trip.

In my architecture and engineering class in eighth grade, I learned a valuable lesson about how well teamwork helps lighten the workload. My teacher asked one of the young ladies to lie down on a table. The rest of our class surrounded her and the table by making a circle. We got as close to the table as possible. My teacher then told us that we were going to pick her up, but by using only our pointer fingers. I thought, *I'm not so sure this is going to work.* Well, I was proven wrong. We picked her up with each person using only one finger. I was shocked at how easily we accomplished the task of lifting her off the table. This story has always stuck with me.

Even though I've preferred to do tasks on my own because I wanted them done a certain way, much more can be accomplished with a team effort. I learned the art of teamwork as I participated in baseball and basketball games growing up. There might be an all-star player on a team, but there's really no such thing as a one-man team. Certainly there are key players who do more than the average teammate, but the coach expects each player to be a team player. This was the case for our mission team.

There were eleven teammates on our trip. We were all given certain tasks to do along the way, and we all wore several hats to make things work. Aaron, Greg, Dave, and I were the cyclists. Our job was to physically train to build up the endurance, strength, and stamina to succeed. Some trained more than others, but we all prepared for the trip. We purchased the proper equipment for the journey, figured out which snacks worked best while cycling on the road, and made adjustments to our bicycles for comfort.

Howard and Kevin were our drivers and maintenance men. They drove from Roanoke, Virginia, to the beach in San Diego, California, to St. Augustine, Florida, and back to Roanoke. It totaled about 7,000 miles of driving. That's a lot of driving. I did relieve them one day in Oklahoma when we were driving to California. I told them that I'd be glad to give them a break one of those days, although I made it clear to them that I wasn't going to back up the motor home since it had a trailer hooked up to it. At the time, I had never backed up with a trailer, and I wasn't about to do it with someone else's RV. Kevin and Howard also took care of the lodging arrangements when we stayed in campgrounds and RV parks. I made as many reservations as possible, but most of the places we stayed did not accept reservations. They were strictly on a first-come, first-served basis. Kevin and Howard also helped out with our bicycle mechanical issues and assisted in other ways, as needed. Without those two, our trip would not have gone as smoothly as it did.

Mindy, Hannah, Elisabeth, and Andrea were on the meal

preparation and laundry team. I knew the cyclists would be too exhausted to help cook after riding one hundred miles, so we recruited a support crew. These team members developed meal plans for each day of the trip. Our team stayed as close as possible to the planned menu, but there were some days when we deviated from it. It was the responsibility of the meal team to make sure our refrigerator, cabinets, and counters were stocked with food and drinks. We mainly drank water, but chocolate almond milk was my go-to drink after a long, hot day of cycling.

These women refilled our water bottles and provided snacks during our breaks. Many times, our snacks were similar to meals. Two to four almond butter and honey sandwiches or a 32-ounce smoothie was my snack most days. One of the toughest jobs was washing the dirty laundry. Can you imagine the disgusting smell of those clothes after riding one hundred miles? Yeah, I'm sure it reeked big time. These ladies even washed our clothes by hand a time or two. God bless them. They also assumed the responsibility of writing thank-you cards to each of the churches, taking pictures, playing music, and other things needed along the way. Without them, our trip would not have been successful.

David (Dave's oldest son) traveled with us to help out with media. I like to think that they had some great bonding moments along the trip. David definitely assisted his dad in many ways. He not only took great photographs, but he also captured some cool video clips and posted updates on social media. He even helped out with meal preparation and laundry detail on occasion. David served in all the churches by leading music, singing specials, presenting his testimony, assisting with the product table, and various other tasks. It was a blessing having him with us, and the trip would not have been successful or as fun without him.

In order for these eleven members to join the mission team, they were required to write their testimony (summarized to one page). There were a few reasons why I wanted them to do this. First of all, I wanted them to be able to clearly share their testimony of salvation. Secondly,

I informed them that they would be asked to share their testimony at some point along the journey. Thirdly, I wanted each of them to always be prepared to share their testimony without hesitation. Dave, Greg, Aaron, Howard, Kevin, David, Mindy, Hannah, Elisabeth, Andrea, and I all shared our testimonies on this mission trip, and I was always encouraged when I heard them.

Please know that there were many times on this trip when each team member went above and beyond the call of duty. We cyclists put our bodies through much agony to accomplish our goal, and the support team did everything they could to make us as comfortable as possible. Each team member did their part so our team could successfully cycle across America.

Ephesians 4:11–12 says, "And he gave some, apostles; and some, prophets; and some, evangelists; and some, pastors and teachers; for the perfecting of the saints, for the work of the ministry, for the edifying of the body of Christ." Not everyone is called to be an apostle (a "sent one"). Not every believer is called to become a missionary overseas. Not every Christian will become a prophet or proclaimer of God's Word. Not everybody is summoned to become an evangelist. God doesn't call every follower to become a pastor or a Bible teacher. Be assured, however, that God has a calling on every one of His children.

Each mission-team member was accountable for a specific task during our adventure across America. Similarly, God has personal assignments for every Christian. He wants us to do great and mighty things. He desires to use us to reach the multitudes with the gospel of Christ. God wants every one of His followers to be actively involved in sharing the gospel of Jesus Christ. Every person has a job to do. God can use you to do the impossible. He can use you to do the incomprehensible. He can use you to accomplish the unattainable. He can use you to do the unthinkable. God wants you on His team. He desires for you to be in the game, not on the sidelines. Far too many self-proclaimed Christians are on the sidelines telling everybody what they should do and how they should do it. If you're on God's team, His church, then He wants you to get busy working where He's called you to work. Always be a team player!

CHAPTER 12

Florida: The Mission of the Church Is Missions

After a relaxing morning observing the Perdido Bay and eating a nice breakfast, our team entered Florida on Friday, June 26, 2015. I'll never forget crossing the bridge over the bay to begin cycling through our final state. It gave me an extra boost of energy and excitement. The final state had come at last, and the lesson God showed me in this state is that the mission of the church is missions.

DIVINE APPOINTMENTS

On Saturday, June 27, I got an early start with the goal of riding as many miles as possible before the support team caught up to me. We had some commitments that evening, and I couldn't risk a late start. The other fellas took the time to rest their limbs for the last leg of the ride. I was cruising along faster than normal that morning because I was attempting to go as far as possible until the RV caught me.

It was a beautiful, sunny morning. There was not a cloud in the sky, and it wasn't too hot. It was just right. Stroking the pedals in the warm morning sun felt transfiguring. The fields on both sides of the road were giving a vibe of peaceful tranquility. It was almost like a religious experience of worshiping the Lord. As I looked from every angle on the saddle, I marveled at the beauty of God's creation. I began to ponder verses about the lilies of the field and God's provision in my life. It was a God moment, for sure.

All of a sudden I saw a couple of cyclists resting ahead on the side of the road. As I approached them, I decided to stop for a break, introduce myself, and see if they wanted to ride a few miles together. I noticed the saddlebags on their bicycles and had a hunch they were riding the Southern Tier like us. Their names were Suzanne and Sadie. To make a long story short, Suzanne was the female cyclist the guy in Arizona had told us about. We had finally caught up to her in Florida, the final state. Sadie was Suzanne's friend and was riding through the state of Florida with her.

Suzanne and Sadie were experienced cyclists who had been riding for many years. We were like newbies compared to them—at least Dave, Aaron, and I were. Greg was the only team member with more experience than us. It was very refreshing to cycle with a couple of new faces. From California to Florida, Dave, Greg, Aaron, and I had pretty much run out of things to talk about. We had exhausted every subject you could think of. It was great for all of us to just have someone else to have a conversation with. After talking with the team, we extended an invitation to them to ride the rest of the state together. They agreed, and it was very enjoyable.

On an overcast day in Florida, we teamed up with Suzanne and Sadie, cruising down the roads of the Florida panhandle. The support team separated from us for a short period of time. They were probably getting gas or groceries. There was hardly any traffic on the roads, but we could see some vehicles in the distance. As we got closer, we realized it was the support team. As we passed each other, we were looking at them like, "Where in the world are you guys going?" The support team had turned around to catch us, so we turned around to catch up to them. Sure enough, we had made a wrong turn a few miles back at a stop sign.

God directed us to Suzanne and Sadie in Florida. These two ladies were a breath of fresh air for our team. It was refreshing meeting new friends and cycling with them. The day I met them, I asked them if they needed anything. If we had it, they were welcome to it. They asked if we had any watermelon, but we didn't. Instead, I offered them some sandwiches. I remember telling Howard that I needed six sandwiches, with four of them being for the ladies I had just met on the road. The RV finally caught up to us, and Sadie and Suzanne were amazed by our support team.

It was another long day for us, and the other cyclists were resting in the morning before finishing up the day. Seeing those two ladies ride inspired our entire team to press on. Everything was going well for us, but we needed a morale booster. Suzanne and Sadie helped our team regain enthusiasm in the state of Florida. Honestly, we were drained and ready to be done, but seeing the joy they had in their adventure reminded us of our purpose.

After some challenging life events, Suzanne set out in May 2015 to cycle across the Southern Tier. She stayed in hotels along the way and had some saddlebags to carry her belongings. A cyclist in Arizona told us about her, and we finally caught up to her in Florida. Sadie, Suzanne's friend, joined her in Florida to finish out the trip. After trying to outrun a thunderstorm with them, our team asked them to join us for the last few rides. They agreed, and we rode into St. Augustine, Florida, together. On June 30, 2015, we even shared our final meal with them at a local St. Augustine restaurant. God sovereignly directed our mission team to them, and we were so grateful to God for allowing our lives to cross paths on such a crazy cycling voyage.

We were cycling along with the two ladies and drafting each other. It was our routine to report any debris, rocks, gravel, bumps, potholes, or anything else that was on the roads. We'd either shout something like "Gravel on your left" or just point to the right or left. I remember saying "Diaper on your left!" Yes, diapers are not the typical artifact you'd find on the side of the road. It was the only one we saw the entire trip. For some reason, Dave thought this was hysterical. He started laughing—like really, really laughing. He was laughing so hard that his abdominal muscles began to hurt, and he began to make odd noises. I began to laugh as well, not necessarily at the diaper, but at how hard

Dave was laughing. I guess you could say that laughter is contagious. I was laughing so hard that my stomach began to hurt and I could barely breathe. I laughed until I cried. Everybody else began to laugh, too, because we were laughing. Maybe we had passed a tank that was blowing out some laughing gas. I don't know. All I do know is if we ever wanted a good laugh throughout Florida, all we had to say was "Diaper on your left."

There is no such thing as coincidences; there are just providential, divine appointments. It was a divine appointment, set up by God Almighty, for us to meet the two ladies on this trip. God used them to encourage us during our time of discouragement, and I pray that our team did the same for them. Take full advantage of every divine appointment God sets in place for you. Capitalize on every opportunity to share God's love and the gospel of Jesus Christ!

AMERICA NEEDS JESUS

We were in Quincy, Florida, when I heard one of the most powerful sermons of the entire trip. Sometimes the churches would have us minister, but other times they would only allow us to serve in other ways. I'm very grateful that we did not provide the message at Thomas Memorial Baptist Church, because Pastor Rob Coram preached an outstanding sermon from Colossians. During his sermon he said these words: "America needs Jesus."

Certainly this is nothing too profound or theological, but it is the simple truth. You have to understand that we finally made it to Florida and were getting weary in well doing. Well, at least I was. Those three words, "America needs Jesus," reiterated the importance of our trip. The purpose of our trip was not only to cycle across America. While that was a great goal, it certainly wasn't our only ambition. Our goal was to capture the world's attention so we could share the message of salvation. Galatians 6:9 says, "And let us not be weary in well doing: for in due season we shall reap, if we faint not." I needed this reminder because it refueled my spiritual desire to continue carrying the gospel torch on the last leg of our journey.

We all had matching cycling jerseys. The front said, "Biking the USA for Yahweh." This identity is what set us apart from all other cross-country cycling groups. We did not identify ourselves with a bike shop, cycling team, etc. Our identity was in Jesus Christ. The back of the jersey had Acts 16:31: "Believe on the Lord Jesus Christ, and thou shalt be saved." We wanted the message of salvation to be very clear and concise on our jerseys. We wanted to have matching jerseys so that people would see that we were a cycling team and were riding together.

Hopefully, having that verse of Scripture on our backs motivated people to read the gospel, whether they saw us as they were driving down the road, walking on the sidewalk, or anywhere else. Romans 10:17 says, "So then faith cometh by hearing, and hearing by the word of God." The only way to hear the gospel is if you read God's Word or hear somebody refer to it. In addition to our cycling jerseys, we also had specially designed T-shirts with the same Bible verse, Acts 16:31, on the back. Our goal was to stand out in the crowd and encourage conversations about Christ's glorious news of salvation, sharing that news with others.

There's no question that America needs Jesus. It is my firm belief that people having a personal relationship with Jesus Christ will solve the vast majority of the problems in America. The world refuses to do the work God has called believers to do. In fact, even many Christians refuse to do the work of evangelism. In 2 Timothy 4:1–5, Paul commanded Timothy to preach the Word in season and out of season and to do the work of an evangelist. Evangelism is not God's suggestion; it's His divine commandment. Without Jesus Christ, the citizens of America and of all other nations will spend eternity in a horrible place called hell. America needs Jesus Christ more than anything the world has to offer. Mankind needs Jesus Christ more than the air they breathe, the water they drink, and the food they eat. Every person needs a personal relationship with Jesus Christ.

BE A WITNESS: CAPTURE THE WORLD'S ATTENTION AND SHARE THE MESSAGE OF SALVATION

Five different times, the New Testament records Jesus Christ commissioning the disciples to go into the world to proclaim the good news of salvation. Here are the verses:

> 1. Go ye therefore, and teach all nations, baptizing them in the name of the Father, and of the Son, and of the Holy Ghost: teaching them to observe all things whatsoever I have commanded you: and, lo, I am with you alway, even unto the end of the world. Amen. **(Matthew 28:19–20)**
>
> 2. And he said unto them, Go ye into all the world, and preach the gospel to every creature. **(Mark 16:15)**
>
> 3. And he said unto them, These are the words which I spake unto you, while I was yet with you, that all things must be fulfilled, which were written in the law of Moses, and in the prophets, and in the psalms, concerning me. Then opened he their understanding, that they might understand the scriptures, and said unto them, Thus it is written, and thus it behooved Christ to suffer, and to rise from the dead the third day: and that repentance and remission of sins should be preached in his name among all nations, beginning at Jerusalem. And ye are witnesses of these things. And, behold, I send the promise of my Father upon you: but tarry ye in the city of

Jerusalem, until ye be endued with power from on high.
(Luke 24:44–49)

4. Then the same day at evening, being the first day of the week, when the doors were shut where the disciples were assembled for fear of the Jews, came Jesus and stood in the midst, and saith unto them, Peace be unto you. **(John 20:19)**

5. But ye shall receive power, after that the Holy Ghost is come upon you: and ye shall be witnesses unto me both in Jerusalem, and in all Judaea, and in Samaria, and unto the uttermost part of the earth. **(Acts 1:8)**

One of the easiest ways to be a witness for Christ is by wearing T-shirts that promote salvation. All you have to do is walk into a store, business, school, etc., and people will read your shirt. As each of the team members had a T-shirt with Acts 16:31 on the back and the cyclists also had jerseys with the same verse on the back, there is no telling how many people were reached through this method. I remember one training ride from Roanoke to Covington, Virginia, when a few people saw our jerseys and the signs on our vehicles. The people stopped to see what we were doing. It was fascinating to watch. Multiple times on that training ride, some of the team members were able to share what we were doing and why we were doing it. Similar things occurred many times while we were cycling across America.

Another way we were privileged to witness for Christ was by passing out gospel literature that briefly shared the purpose of our trip and included a presentation of the gospel message. Whenever we went into a grocery store, gas station, or church service, or met someone along the way, we passed out the literature. Only heaven will reveal the eternal impact of those gospel tracts.

One of the greatest ways to be a witness for Christ is by engaging in personal conversations with people. I don't remember a whole lot about Safford, Arizona, but there are a few things that stand out. I will never forget the crazy headwind and cycling well over one hundred miles. It was grueling and exhausting, and I was tempted to throw in the towel. I even ran out of water several miles before arriving at the church in Safford. The address I had on my phone wasn't the right one, and by the time I got to our destination, it was dark and well past 9:00 p.m.

When I finally pulled into the church parking lot, I was very thirsty and extremely hungry. The team said we were going to walk to a local restaurant to eat. Hold on! Imagine cycling around 120 miles, arriving at your destination, and someone tells you to walk down the road a mile or two to eat. Needless to say, my reaction wasn't the best. Looking back, I know it was the providence of God. We walked into Subway, and I purchased two foot-long subs. Yes, that's a lot, but you'd eat that much, too, if you had done what we had done. The cashiers' looks were unforgettable. We began talking to the employees, sharing what we were doing and why we were doing it, and we gave them some gospel tracts. One of them came up to us and donated to our cause. God's providence was manifested that day in our lives, and I'm thankful I didn't refuse to walk to Subway.

I was truly amazed at the prayer support of all the people who were not associated with our church body. Congregations from all across the country prayed for us. Every church where we ministered had a special time of prayer for us while we were there. I gave them a copy of our itinerary, and they promised to pray for us along the way. The schedule contained the number of miles we were traveling, which cities we were staying in, the churches we were involved with, and in which campgrounds we would stay each night. As we promoted this event, people kept track of us through those schedules, and it gave them the opportunity to pray more specifically for us.

When we were in Quincy, Florida, doing a gospel-sing benefit after a long day of riding, a few different groups ministered during the service. We went last. We sang songs, played instruments, and testified about our trip. It made each of us excited that we were in the state of

Florida, only days away from the beach in St. Augustine. Just before the pastor closed the service, another minister suggested they lay hands on us and pray. That was another God moment. We were exhausted, but those prayers brought renewed strength. It was through the prayers of our comrades in the faith that God provided the physical, spiritual, and mental strength to advance the gospel through events like this one.

On the final day of our trip, I may not have been the best witness— at least to my team members. After nearly a month of being gracious and dealing with punctuality issues, I told the guys the night before the last day of our journey that I would be leaving at a certain time the next morning, with or without them. I guess you could say my father was coming out in me. We were scheduled to meet up with those two lady cyclists, along with a local pastor and his son. The next morning, I woke everyone up and reminded them of what time I was leaving. I reiterated that I would be leaving with or without them. I went through the motor home and the church rooms to make sure everyone was awake. I did this three different times, starting about an hour before we were supposed to leave.

My departure time of 8:00 a.m. came, and I took off solo to meet up with the other four cyclists. Please keep in mind that the team had been warned three times. Fortunately, they had access to an extra set of maps in the motor home, and I was texting them turn-by-turn directions along the way. Well, this didn't go over very well with my group. Our last day began with a schism, and I had caused it. Perhaps it was a selfish decision, and maybe I should have waited just a few more minutes. If I could do it all over again, I would have delayed leaving so that we all could have left and traveled together. It was all my fault, and I learned a great lesson. I was consumed with bitterness because of the punctuality issue throughout the trip. My selfish pride got the best of me.

To make matters worse, we couldn't find the entrance to the greenway that was clearly designated on our map for us to ride on. Dave and Aaron eventually caught up to me and the two female cyclists, and Greg somehow found the right entrance to the greenway. I guess Greg was not just a better mechanic, but he was also a better navigator. We finally found the local pastor and his son. I faced the facts, admitted my shortcomings, and apologized. The two female cyclists, the local pastor and son, Aaron, Mindy, Greg, Dave, and I enjoyed the rest of the greenway together before reconnecting with the support team.

∾o∾

WHERE WILL YOU SPEND ETERNITY?

Ten out of ten people die. Hebrews 9:27 says, "It is appointed unto men once to die, but after this the judgment." The Bible reveals that every person will spend eternity either in a glorious place called heaven or in a horrific place called hell. *Are you 100 percent certain that you would spend eternity in heaven if you died today?*

Romans 3:23 says, "For all have sinned, and come short of the glory of God." Every man, woman, boy, and girl who has ever existed, except for Jesus Christ, has sinned and broken God's law. Sin means to miss the mark or to come short of God's perfection. It doesn't matter if we have only told a little white lie or if we have committed the vilest crime imaginable—once we sin, we're instantly separated from God. James 2:10 says that if we keep the entire law but break it in one point, we are guilty of it all. The only way to be reconciled with God is by having a personal relationship with Jesus Christ.

Romans 6:23 says, "For the wages of sin is death." Do you remember your first job? My first job was at Food Lion. I was a cashier and bagger. Let's just say it wasn't my dream job, and I'm glad I moved on, although receiving my first paycheck was awesome. I was sixteen years old, and the check wasn't even for a hundred dollars, but I felt like a big shot depositing it into the bank. The term *wage* means "payment," and the payment for our sin is death. The word *death* certainly means "to die," but it also presents the connotation of eternal separation from God in hell. This is the eternal fate of every person who doesn't put their faith in Jesus Christ. Matthew 25:46 states, "And these shall go away into everlasting punishment."

CHRIST PAID FOR THE PENALTY OF SIN

Romans 5:8 declares, "But God commendeth his love toward us, in that, while we were yet sinners, Christ died for us." *Commendeth* literally means "to approve." God's love was approved and demonstrated two thousand years ago when Christ died on Calvary's cross. It was on the cross where Christ paid our penalty of sin and died in our place. First John 2:1–2 reveals that Christ was not just the propitiation for believers' sins, but He was also the propitiation for the sins of the entire world. When Christ's body was broken, beaten, battered, butchered, and bruised, every sin was charged to His account.

PUT YOUR FAITH AND TRUST IN JESUS CHRIST TODAY

John 3:16 states, "For God so loved the world, that he gave his only begotten Son, that whosoever believeth in him should not perish, but have everlasting life." Believing on Jesus Christ as Savior means to trust in Him alone for salvation. You must have faith that He died on the cross for your sins and that He rose from the grave (Romans 10:9–13). You cannot work your way to heaven, and eternal life is not granted by any other means. Jesus Christ is the only way to heaven. John 14:6 says, "Jesus saith unto him, I am the way, the truth, and the life: no man cometh unto the Father, but by me." Put your faith in Jesus Christ before it's eternally too late.

The last day of our trip certainly did not go how we had planned it, but God opened some opportunities to share the gospel. Aaron, Dave, Greg, and I were joined by the two female cyclists we had met a few days earlier in Florida. They were a breath of fresh air to us and boosted our morale. Honestly, before meeting them we were ready to be done and had lost some of the joy. We turned left onto a main road, but I wasn't sure it was the right one. I decided to get out my phone and maps to verify. Sure enough, it was the right one.

The others were almost half a mile away when I started pedaling again. I crossed a bridge and heard a loud BANG. It sounded like a gunshot, and it scared me to death. I jumped, flinched, and screamed all at the same time. Then I noticed that my tire was coming off my back wheel. It had popped, and thankfully, the RV had just passed me. After Howard and Kevin changed my tire and tube, the others were well out of sight. I stepped up the pace to catch them but never saw them. They stayed with the route on the maps we had purchased, but I stayed on the main road because I saw a sign that said, "St. Augustine 16 miles away." Somehow I got to St. Augustine about an hour before the rest of the team, but I couldn't find the beach.

Can you imagine cycling all the way from San Diego, California, to St. Augustine, Florida, and not being able to find the Atlantic Ocean? None of us could figure out the maps, and we didn't have an address to put in the GPS. I just kept cycling through town and then crossed a bridge in the bay. I looked back, but the RV wasn't in sight. They were attending to some difficulties they were having, so I focused on finding St. Augustine Beach. I saw a lady walking on the sidewalk, but she gave me the cold shoulder when I approached her. Then a cyclist zoomed by me. I caught up to him and said, "Hey. My name is Bryan, and I've cycled across America from San Diego, but I cannot find the beach. Can you help me out?"

He graciously guided me to the beach. Once we got there, I shared with him what I was doing and why. After I shared the gospel with him, he broke down and shared how tough of a time he was having. He was currently homeless and just used his bicycle to travel. I had a bunch of leftover snacks in my back pocket, and I gave them all to him.

I was not sure he'd like them, but it was all I had. I asked if I could pray for him, and he agreed. After I prayed with him, we parted ways.

As I reflect on this memory, I am reminded of God's sovereign hand. It was the providence of God that my tire popped, that I got separated from the team, and that I arrived earlier than the others. If none of that had happened, that man would have never cycled past me.

While waiting for the rest of the team to get to the beach in St. Augustine, I took advantage of the downtime. It was so nice to just sit back, relax, and be done. As the rest of the team approached the beach, they took shelter as a severe thunderstorm unleashed its energy. They were about two hundred yards from where I was, and they found refuge in the storm. I was in a snack shop, and the rain didn't touch me. I was sitting at a table, and a man named Douglas sat down beside me. He was letting the storm pass before going back out to catch more fish. During our conversation, I made a transition to spiritual matters. Douglas was an adamant nonbeliever, but I believe God used our conversation to make him rethink his position. He remarked that he found it hard to believe some portions of the Bible, so I asked him to elaborate. We had a great discussion. I used my apologetics knowledge to explain how God's Word is credible, and then I presented the gospel to him. Even though Douglas did not receive this message, I believe the gospel seed was planted. My prayer is that God will save him before it's eternally too late.

Proverbs 11:30 says, "The fruit of the righteous is a tree of life; and he that winneth souls is wise." Do you wish to be a wise believer? A wise believer is a soul winner. The beauty about sharing the gospel and being a witness for Christ is you don't have to cycle across America or go overseas to do it. You can start by sharing Christ with your family, friends, or anybody else. Just be a witness for Christ. It's your calling from God.

And in the End...

CHAPTER 13
Daily Overview of Our Trip

One of my personal goals was to keep a daily journal of our journey. My regret is that I didn't write everything down each day, although the short journals were used to keep our friends, family, and church members updated. Everything in the "Days" section below is what I wrote at the end of each day for our Facebook page so our followers could be informed with a brief summarization of the mileage, events, and happenings of each day (https://www.facebook.com/BikingtheUSAforYahweh/). You can view each of the rides on my profile on the Strava App: https://www.strava.com/athletes/7985122

We rode a total of 2,910.1 miles across the Southern Tier Route from San Diego, California, to St. Augustine, Florida. We were on bicycles for 191 hours and 20 minutes. We climbed approximately 87,680 feet of elevation gain. That's like hiking up Mount Everest three times.

> **Warm Up:** On Sunday, May 31, 2015, we rode 21.2 miles from Ocean Beach in San Diego, CA, to our motor home park in La Mesa, CA. After some discussion with our support team, we decided it would be much easier to go for a short ride from our official starting point to the RV park. Logistics would have demanded a 4:00 a.m. start, not just for the riders, but also for the support team. We made an afternoon trip out of it, although we weren't able to enjoy much time on the shore because we couldn't find a legal parking spot for the RV. We barely had enough time to get a

group photo. Cruising through the suburbs of San Diego on our bicycles was a wonderful experience.

Day 1: San Diego, CA, to El Centro, CA—110 miles. We climbed more elevation than expected. It was a challenging day. We rode through the hot part of the day, but with God's help, we successfully completed our first day. While we were in El Centro, we stayed in the gymnasium of First Baptist Church. Pastor and Mrs. Rogers have a gospel-centered ministry exalting Christ. If you are ever in El Centro, you need to visit their church. Pastor Rogers treated us for dinner at a local restaurant called Maranatha. For the record, their BBQ sandwiches are good. Please continue to keep us in your prayers.

Day 2: El Centro, CA, to Blythe, CA—113.6 miles. We completed our second day with God's help. Today was a challenging day, but easier than Day 1 because there was not as much elevation gain. This evening we are staying in a campground in Blythe, CA. Thank you all so very much for your prayers and your support. Please continue to pray for us.

Day 3: Our team successfully rode 113.5 miles from Blythe, CA, to Wickenburg, AZ. This evening we are staying on the campus of Calvary Baptist Church. All is going well for our team, and everyone is staying healthy. Thanks be unto the Lord. Hannah, Elisabeth, and Andrea are feeding us well. #Hallelujah Brother Kevin and Brother Howard are doing a splendid job driving and helping the riders throughout the day. Please continue to keep us in your prayers.

Day 4: Our team successfully rode from Wickenburg,

AZ, to Apache Junction, AZ. We took a couple of wrong turns and also made a special detour to In-N-Out Burger for lunch. It lengthened our ride to 103.3 miles, but it was worth it. Today's ride was much easier than the previous three because it was primarily flat. One of Bryan's roommates from Bible college, Jeremiah Winstead, stopped by the RV park for a special time of fellowship. He presented each rider with a special bracelet that increases the pH levels for better athletic performances. Thanks to everyone who is fasting and praying on our behalf. Your comments, texts, messages, and phone calls are inspiring. Please keep us in your prayers as we pedal to promote the gospel of Christ.

Day 5: Our team rode 130 miles from Apache Junction, AZ, to Safford, AZ. Today's average temperature was 76.5 degrees. At the beginning of our ride, it was raining. About twenty miles into the ride the rain ceased, but it remained overcast. Needless to say, today was a wonderful day for a ride. Pastor Bryan had a flat tire, but a new spare tube fixed it right up. We are staying at First Baptist Church of Safford this evening. Thanks to all for your prayers. Please continue to pray for us.

Day 6: We made it to New Mexico. We rode 120 miles from Safford, AZ, to Silver City, NM. Tomorrow morning we will be ministering at the First Baptist Church of Silver City. Please pray that God uses our team to exalt the Savior, evangelize the sinner, and edify the saints.

Day 7: We were given the privilege to minister at the First Baptist Church of Silver City this morning. Brother Dave preached, and our team served in their church for the morning service. If you are ever in Silver City, check out one of their services. Pastor Jason, his family, and the congregation are wonderful folks. After the service, we rode from Silver City, NM, to Caballo, NM—a total of 68.5 miles. The average temperature was 80.6 degrees, with cloudy skies to shade us while we rode. We reached our highest elevation point at 8,200 feet. As you can imagine, we were excited about reaching the peak because it concluded the last major climb of our journey. This evening we are staying at a campground in Caballo. Please continue to keep us in your prayers.

Day 8: Today we rode 74.4 miles from Caballo, NM, to Las Cruces, NM. We just finished ministering at a block party and gospel illusion show at East Mesa Baptist Church. If you are ever in Las Cruces, you should visit this church. Pastor Jim and the people of East Mesa Baptist are awesome. Please continue to pray for us as we travel to Fort Hancock, Texas, tomorrow.

Day 9: We rode 98.1 miles from Las Cruces, NM, to Fort Hancock, TX. We were able to pass out many tracts/pamphlets today. We are staying at the Fort Hancock Motel this evening. Tomorrow we will be at the Wednesday evening service of Van Horn Community Church. Please pray that God will use our team to edify the saints and evangelize the sinners. Thanks to each of you for your continued prayers.

Day 10: Today we have finished one-third of our journey across the country. To date, we have ridden 1,028.1 miles, climbed 40,368 feet of elevation, and spent 72 hours and 32 minutes riding a bicycle. Today we rode 73.5 miles from Fort Hancock, TX, to Van

Horn, TX. This evening we were able to minister at Van Horn Community Church. The team sang praises, gave testimonies, and proclaimed the Word of God. Please pray for Pastor Rodney as he ministers in the Van Horn community. Thanks to each of you for your continued prayers.

Day 11: We safely arrived in Alpine, Texas, after 103 miles of riding. We are getting ready to eat some dinner. Thanks to all of you for your prayers. As many of you know, this trip has a twofold purpose: (1) Raising gospel awareness in the USA and (2) Raising money for the building fund of Clearbrook Baptist Church. Please specifically pray that God would continue to open doors for us to share the gospel. Also, please prayerfully consider sponsoring our team financially. Feel free to make your contribution online at www.bikingtheusa.org.[9] May God richly bless you with a great evening.

Day 12: We successfully rode 86.7 miles from Alpine, TX, to Sanderson, TX. We served at First Calvary Baptist Church by singing, testifying, and sharing some gospel illusions. We also enjoyed the great food. We are staying in the church's cottage this evening. Thanks for your continued prayers.

Day 13: This morning we went to breakfast with Pastor and Mrs. Welch from the church we were at yesterday. The day started off as a dream for a cyclist in the desert because it was overcast and misting; however, as the day progressed, the weather became a nightmare. For the last seventy or eighty miles of our 120-mile day, we encountered a troubling headwind. Headwinds make cyclists work harder with little results. With that said,

---

[9.] This option is no longer available.

we safely made it to the First Baptist Church of Del Rio, Texas, where we will be serving tomorrow. Please keep us in your prayers.

Day 14: Today we praise the Lord for the opportunity to serve in the junior church of the First Baptist Church of Del Rio. After church, we all enjoyed some Chinese food at a local restaurant. We did not ride today because it was our rest day. Thank you for your continued prayers. Hannah and Andrea safely arrived in Roanoke, Virginia. Aaron and Mindy Wallace will join us tomorrow evening for the rest of our journey. Please keep us in your prayers.

Day 15: We rode 98.9 miles from Del Rio, TX, to Leakey, TX. We said goodbye to our friends at the First Baptist Church of Del Rio. At the end of our ride, we encountered a downpour of rain right as we entered Leakey. We stayed in a cabin reserved by Aaron and Mindy Wallace. Sorry for the delay in the updates. We literally went 150 miles without any cell phone signal. Thanks for your continued prayers.

Day 16: We rode 88.1 miles from Leakey, TX, to Fredericksburg, TX. Today was Aaron's first ride and Mindy's first day helping with the support team. Both did outstanding jobs. Today's ride consisted of rain, rain, and more rain, but we thanked God for keeping the temperature cooler than normal. We are staying in a nice RV park tonight. Please continue to keep us in your prayers.

Day 17: With help from Almighty God, our team successfully rode 111.9 miles from Fredericksburg, TX, to Bastrop, TX. We were unable to schedule a church service today, although God opened up several opportunities to witness and pass out our tracts. Thanks for your continued prayers. May God richly bless you with a great evening.

Day 18: We rode 50.9 miles from Bastrop, TX, to Round Top, TX. We encountered much rainfall and were forced to make a decision to shorten our day. The scattered thunderstorm showers were too risky to ride through. We praise the Lord that this is the first time we have detoured from our schedule. The next two days we will make up for lost time. When we stopped in Round Top, we decided to go to the Round Top Café, and the gentleman waiting our table gave us free food. Hallelujah! Chocolate-chip pie and apple pie never tasted so good. Please continue to pray for us. May God's richest blessings be upon each of you.

Day 19: Today we rode 124 miles from Round Top, TX, to Coldspring, TX. God proved to be faithful to us once again. While stopping at a gas station to take a brief break, we met a nice young man named Forrest. He approached us to compliment our Christian bike jerseys. We proceeded to share with him what we were doing, and we gave him one of our pamphlets. Forrest then prayed with us inside the gas station. #PrayerWorks What an encouragement it was to meet a young man in Texas who was not ashamed to pray in public. Please continue to pray for us as we embark on the longest day of our journey tomorrow.

Day 20: Our team successfully rode 151 miles from Coldspring, TX, to DeRidder, LA. We are two-thirds finished with our journey. We are thankful for the opportunity to serve in Pleasant Hill Baptist Church in DeRidder. We are back on our schedule after today's extensive ride. Thanks to each of you for your faithful prayers. May God richly bless you with a great evening.

Day 21: We were given the opportunity to meet Pastor Danny, his wife, Susan, and many of the wonderful members of Pleasant Hill Baptist Church. We were so grateful for the three meals they prepared for us and the opportunity to minister in Sunday school and during the morning worship service. After the service, we rode ninety-seven miles to Bunkie, LA, where we met some of the members of First Baptist Church. They gave us pizza for dinner (yes, it was good). Thanks for your continued prayers. May God richly bless you with a great evening.

Day 22: Today we said goodbye to the folks at the First Baptist Church of Bunkie, LA. Pastor Mark, Sister Faye, and all the many members were very hospitable and generous to us. We praise the Lord for the strength to have ridden 87.6 miles to St Francisville, LA. Mindy and Elisabeth deserve much credit today because they noticed that we made a wrong turn. Had we continued in that direction, we would have been many miles off the route. While riding today, we encountered some mechanical problems (flat tires) and some other issues that prohibited us from going to Jackson, LA. As a result, we are staying in a hotel. God is in control. Please keep us in your prayers as we make up lost mileage tomorrow.

Day 23: We rode 89.4 miles from Francisville, LA, to Franklinton, LA. We are staying this evening at a state park. We are slightly off schedule but will be back on track tomorrow, Lord willing. Thanks to everyone who has been praying for us. God supernaturally shielded us from a rough thunderstorm, and we rode the entire day without any flat tires.

Day 24: Today we encountered some severe thunderstorms, and now we are about sixty miles behind schedule. We rode about seventy miles, from Franklinton, LA, to Wiggins, MS. We are very thankful to the Lord for keeping us safe, as a terrible storm came out of nowhere. We were privileged to attend the service of Magnolia Springs Assembly of God, and were blessed to have met Pastor Keith and his sweet wife. Please pray for us as we attempt to make up lost mileage tomorrow. Lord willing, we will enter into Florida tomorrow.

Day 25: Today we rode 142.9 miles from Wiggins, MS, to Lillian, AL. We were honored to visit a godly woman named Mrs. Scott, who fixed us a wonderful lunch. We met her in New Mexico while ministering in a church. Thanks for your continued prayers. May God richly bless you with a great evening.

Day 26: With the help of Almighty God, we rode ninety-eight miles from Lillian, AL, to DeFuniak Springs, Florida. Today we would like to give a special shout-out to Kevin Dunbar and Howard for being the best RV drivers. They have been working hard making sure we have a safe place to sleep, helping us navigate the route, and making sure our bicycles are good to ride. Thanks to all of you for your continued prayers and support. Only four more days left until we will reach the beach on the East Coast. May God richly bless you with a great day.

Day 27: Today we rode 111.2 miles from DeFuniak Springs, FL, to Quincy, FL. While riding, we met up with two ladies who are riding the same cross-country route. It was really neat to ride with them for sixty miles of the ride. After our ride, we ministered in Santa Clara Baptist Church. We had a wonderful gospel sing and enjoyed meeting Pastor and Mrs. Adams and the kind folks in the area. Tomorrow morning we will be involved in the services of Thomas Memorial Baptist Church. Thanks to all for your continued prayers. May God richly bless you with a great evening.

Day 28: Today we rode 85.3 miles from Quincy, FL, to Madison, FL. We were privileged to be involved in the morning services of Thomas Memorial Baptist Church. Pastor Rob preached a powerful message from Colossians 2. We have two days of riding left. #Hallelujah #PTL #Amen Please continue to keep our team in prayer as we ride to Gainesville, Florida, tomorrow. May God richly bless you with a great day.

Day 29: We rode 125.2 miles from Madison, FL, to Gainesville, FL. We were joined by two ladies who were also riding the Southern Tier. We will ride with them tomorrow as well. We are staying this evening on the property of Westside Baptist Church. Please continue to keep us in your prayers. We would like to give a special shout-out to four special ladies: Mindy, Hannah, Elisabeth, and Andrea. These ladies have done a tremendous job keeping us fed, shopping, preparing meals, doing laundry, and many other things throughout our trip. Tomorrow is our last day. Please pray that we finish strong.

Day 30: Today we rode 90.7 miles from Gainesville, FL to St. Augustine, FL. We give God the glory for allowing us the strength, courage, and boldness to accomplish this trip. Please pray for our safety as we travel back to Roanoke tomorrow.

CHAPTER 14

Lessons Learned

This trip taught me that anything can be accomplished with determination, perspiration, and divine intervention. If we seek God's help, work hard, and adopt the right mind-set, we can complete any task we set our minds to.

THE LESSON OF DETERMINATION

One of the greatest lessons I personally learned on this trip was that of determination. With enough determination, we can accomplish anything we set our minds to. There's no doubt that attitude determines altitude. Our faith will soar with altitude when we determine to have the right attitude. I heard a preacher say this profound statement sometime back: "Outlook determines outcome." Whenever we determine to adopt a positive outlook, we will achieve a positive outcome. This goes beyond simply positive thinking, although positive thinking can accomplish profound wonders in each of our lives. It's about the right mindset.

I believe our mindset about life is what will make it or break it. The right mindset will help us achieve our goals, dreams, and ambitions. You truly can accomplish anything you set your mind to, as long as it's accompanied with determination. If God was able to provide our team with the ability to complete the rigorous task of cycling across America, then surely He can do similar things for you. What does God want you to determine to do with the rest of your life?

Years ago, after I meditated in the Word, God revealed to me the importance of making the determination to live my life for Him.

> Wherefore seeing we also are compassed about with so great a cloud of witnesses, let us lay aside every weight, and the sin which doth so easily beset us, and let us run with patience the race that is set before us, looking unto Jesus the author and finisher of our faith; who for the joy that was set before him endured the cross, despising the shame, and is set down at the right hand of the throne of God. (Hebrews 12:1–2)

Determine today that you are going to look unto Jesus and live a life of faith for His glory!

THE LESSON OF PERSPIRATION

"Hard work beats talent when talent does not work hard." That is a philosophy that several of my coaches instilled in me growing up. I may not have been the best athlete on the court or field, but I was willing to work the hardest. This trip reminded me of the importance of working hard and being willing to perspire to accomplish a goal. Nothing of great significance is ever accomplished without hard work! Colossians 3:23–24 says, "And whatsoever ye do, do it heartily, as to the Lord, and not unto men; knowing that of the Lord ye shall receive the reward of the inheritance: for ye serve the Lord Christ."

Did you know that laziness is something God is displeased with? Proverbs 6:6–8 says, "Go to the ant, thou sluggard; consider her ways, and be wise: which having no guide, overseer, or ruler, provideth her meat in the summer, and gathereth her food in the harvest." The Holy Spirit provides an example of working hard from an ant, of all creatures. No matter the season of life, ants are willing to work hard to finish whatever task they are given by their queen.

In like manner, God expects us to do our very best whenever, wherever, or whatever He calls us to. One pastor said it this way: "Do your best, and God will do the rest." If we do our very best, then God will take care of the rest! Be willing to do every task life brings you as if you are doing it for Almighty God. With that in mind, one could do their very best in life to follow God's Word, but that doesn't guarantee an eternity in heaven. Salvation is only obtained by entrusting Jesus Christ as your personal Lord and Savior, and by faith, believing His sacrifice is the atonement for sin and believing in His resurrection. Jesus Christ was sent into the world about two thousand years ago to offer the very best sacrifice on the cross. He abolished death, hell, and the grave. God is now calling every Christian to live their life as a sacrifice for Him. Romans 12:1–2 says, "I beseech you therefore, brethren, by the mercies of God, that ye present your bodies a living sacrifice, holy, acceptable unto God, which is your reasonable service. And be not conformed to this world: but be ye transformed by the renewing of your mind, that ye may prove what is that good, and acceptable, and perfect, will of God."

The Lesson of Divine Intervention

Time and time again across America, God reminded me of how He divinely intervenes on behalf of His children. God demonstrated His intervention on our behalf in countless ways, such as when we were stranded in a thunderstorm in Mississippi, when I was escorted across a two-mile bridge in Texas, when we got turned around with directions, when we missed our turns along the way, and when we experienced incredible generosity from all the churches. Romans 8:28 comes to mind when I reflect on this. It says, "And we know that all things work together for good to them that love God, to them who are the called according to his purpose."

The same God who divinely intervened for Moses and the Israelites at the Red Sea crossing, for Daniel in the lions' den, for Elijah on Mount Carmel, and for the vast hungry crowd with five loaves of bread and two small fish is the same God today, and He can divinely intervene in your life. No matter the circumstance or situation, God is the omniscient, omnipresent, omnipotent God who performs the miracle of intervention.

This trip taught me that you don't have to be a super saint to receive His interceding aid. Your name does not have to be mentioned in the Bible. You don't have to be one of the Old Testament prophets or one of the twelve disciples in the New Testament. You don't have to be a pastor of a giant megachurch or have a seminary education. All you have to do is ask Him for His help, and He will do it! From this moment forward, commit to asking God for His interceding intervention in your life. Psalm 46:1 says, "God is our refuge and strength, a very present help in trouble."

CONCLUSION

As I reflect upon this cycling adventure, I am truly amazed at the grace of God. The apostle Paul said, "But by the grace of God I am what I am" (1 Corinthians 15:10). If it hadn't been for God's grace and mercy, we would have never accomplished this task. God wants to use you to do something big in and through you. We give all glory, honor, and praise to God for providing us the strength and stamina to ride from coast to coast.

As I reflect upon this trip, I am reminded that with God all things are possible. Jesus said, "With men this is impossible; but with God all things are possible" (Matthew 19:26). If God is able to save to the uttermost and help us ride from coast to coast, then I firmly believe God can do something great and mighty in your life as well. God wants to use you. The impossible is possible with God.

As I reflect upon this trip, I am reminded of Ephesians 3:20: "Now unto him that is able to do exceeding abundantly above all that we ask or think, according to the power that worketh in us." We asked God to help us on this cycling trip, and He did more than we could have imagined. God can do the same for you.

Thank you for supporting our cause by purchasing this book. All the royalties and proceeds are going toward the building fund of Clearbrook Baptist Church. We are truly blessed by each individual who has generously and graciously helped our cause. Please pray that God will provide the finances so we can expand our facilities. We believe that God will supply our every need. "But my God shall supply all your need according to his riches in glory by Christ Jesus" (Philippians 4:19).

NOW WHAT?

One of my favorite hymns is called "Blessed Assurance." Here are the beautiful lyrics:

Verse 1:
Blessed assurance, Jesus is mine!
Oh, what a foretaste of glory divine!
Heir of salvation, purchase of God,
Born of His Spirit, washed in His blood.

Chorus:
This is my story, this is my song,
Praising my Savior all the day long;
This is my story, this is my song,
Praising my Savior all the day long.

Verse 2:
Perfect submission, perfect delight!
Visions of rapture now burst on my sight;
Angels descending bring from above
Echoes of mercy, whispers of love.

Verse 3:
Perfect submission, all is at rest,
I in my Savior am happy and blest;
Watching and waiting, looking above,
Filled with His goodness, lost in His love.

The word *assurance* means "a positive declaration intended to give confidence; a promise." God has given us the greatest promise—eternal life with Him in heaven. Now what? you might be asking. Now is the time to get off our blessed assurances and advance the gospel of Jesus Christ. God is calling us to proclaim His Word and to do the work of an evangelist! May God help us all to advance His gospel into the world!

> I charge thee therefore before God, and the Lord Jesus Christ, who shall judge the quick and the dead at his appearing and his kingdom; *Preach the word; be instant in season, out of season;* reprove, rebuke, exhort with all long suffering and doctrine. For the time will come when they will not endure sound doctrine; but after their own lusts shall they heap to themselves teachers, having itching ears; and they shall turn away their ears from the truth, and shall be turned unto fables. But watch thou in all things, endure afflictions, *do the work of an evangelist,* make full proof of thy ministry. (2 Timothy 4:1–5, emphasis added)

Order Information

REDEMPTION ℙ
P R E S S

To order additional copies of this book, please visit
www.redemption-press.com.
Also available on Amazon.com and BarnesandNoble.com
Or by calling toll-free 1-844-2REDEEM.